Published by: G.W. Kent, Inc.
3667 Morgan Rd.
Ann Arbor, MI 48108 U.S.A.

Copyright © Amateur Winemaker Publications Ltd. 1985

1st Impression 1976
2nd Impression 1977
3rd Impression 1979
4th Impression 1981
5th Impression 1982
6th Impression 1985
Revised edition 1985
8th Impression 1993

ISBN 0-9619072-1-5

Printed in the United States of America

HOW TO LIVE TO 120!

I were brought up on cider
And I be a hundred and two
But still that be 'nuthin when you come to think
Me father and mother be still in the pink
And they were brought up on cider
Of the rare old Tavistock brew
And me Granfer drinks quarts
For he's one of the sports
That were brought up on cider too.

– Old Devonshire chorus

CONTENTS

Foreword

It is sometimes said that the convert is more enthusiastic and zealous than one born in the faith, and it occurs to me that the same might be said of our author—that she is more committed to the cause of cider than many who were born in apple-producing areas. Jo Deal's interest in cider was aroused when some years ago she moved from the Home Counties to Devon and she has been studying the subject intensively both there and on the Continent ever since.

No West Countryman will need persuading of the virtues of cider, if lesser breeds might, for it has a tradition stretching back into the mists of time, and is part of the living Celtic folk culture on both sides of the Channel, in Somerset, Devon and Cornwall and in Normandy and Brittany. In these regions cider, in one form or another, whether "scrumpy" or "cidre dur" has always been the popular drink with the country folk, and figured largely in their cuisine.

In recent years, however, thanks largely to the excellent ciders now being produced commercially in Britain, there has been a great revival in cider drinking particularly among the younger generation until its popularity now bids fair to parallel that of lager. It is only natural, therefore, that with apples so readily and often freely available one's thoughts should turn to making it in some quantity at home.

This book will show you how.

Jo Deal is an acknowledged expert on the subject and the cider she and her husband make—in domestic quantities within anyone's capabilities—is superb, as I can personally testify! You can have equal success by following her recipes. The same is true of her cookery recipes which are both practical and delicious. For good measure she includes a wealth of useful information on cider history, on commercial cider, on apple and cider types, on equipment and where to obtain it, and on sources of supply.

As a keen advocate for many years of the greater use of our native apple for wine making, cookery and, most especially cider, I find this book both fascinating and useful—as no doubt will you.

C. J. J. BERRY

CHAPTER 1

A Little History

Drink up thee cider, George
Pass us round the mug.
Drink up thee cider, George
The garden's ver'nigh dug.
Thy cheeks are getting redder,
From Chaterhouse to Cheddar,
But there's still more cider in the jug.

This is the first verse of an old country song that is still sung at many social gatherings in the West Country, especially around harvest time when a "mug of cider" is really appreciated.

Cider (from the Anglo-Saxon "Seider") is an ancient drink made, of course, from apples, and there are many versions of how it first came to be introduced to this country.

Some books say it was the Phoenicians, who traded in tin with the Cornish people, who were responsible, and it seems likely that by the time of the Roman occupation cider was available, for at that time the town that preceded the modern Glastonbury was known as "Avallonia", meaning "apple orchard". And if they had apples, it is highly unlikely that they did not also have cider.

Other authorities claim that cider was first introduced into Britain by the monks of Forde Abbey, near Axminster, in Devon, soon after the Norman conquest in 1066. This is equally credible, for large quantities of both and sweet dry cider were then – and still are – made in apple-growing Normandy, where it is used a great deal in cooking, often replacing white wine used elsewhere in France. In

1588 a galleon of the Spanish Armada, named Calvados, foundered on a group of rocks in a bay opposite Le Havre, from which the department of Calvados is so called. The brandy Calvados, which is distilled from the cider of Normandy, and made in this area, takes its name from the region. The best Calvados is said to be made in the Vallee-d'Auge and has a high alcoholic content. It is interesting to note that in France, by law, cider should not contain less than 3.5 per cent alcohol by volume.

There are many ancient beliefs and customs associated with the apple. In the early 17th century, the wassailing of apple trees was a form of salutation performed annually by farmers and their workers. (The phrase Wassail or "Wass Hal" means "Be thou of good health"). The date of this ceremony appears to have varied from

area to area; in some it took place on Christmas Eve, in others on Twelfth Night. The farmers and farm workers are said to have carried jugs of cider into the apple orchards, and after drinking a health to the trees and the following year's crop, the remains of the cider were poured around the roots of the trees. During the wassailing much noise was created by the banging of pots and pans, and later, with the introduction of guns, volleys of shots were fired instead. Wheat flour cakes were quite often eaten at these ceremonies and small pieces of cake were dipped in cider and placed in the forks of the trees, probably as a thanksgiving to the spirit of the trees.

Although cider has such a long history, there came a time when its popularity began to decline, possibly due to the introduction of cheap spirit, but by the early 19th century cider making had once again become a profitable business.

One of the first varieties of apples sold in this country was the Costard, and in olden times people who sold apples were called Costard Mongers and this is the derivation of the name coster-monger still given to hawkers of fruit.

There appears to be a growing interest amongst amateur cider makers in the area of Devon where we live. Several orchards are being replanted with more recent varieties of trees suitable for cider making, the names of which I have mentioned in Chapter 3. One farmer recently revived the custom of wassailing the apple trees and this aroused much interest locally.

When we first started making cider we visited many local farmers who were cider makers, listening to their yarns, tasting their brews and at the same time gathering much information. Although not many of them were interested in how cider was introduced into this country so many years ago, they were only too eager to talk about their fathers and grandfathers who had also been cider makers. We heard many times that cider was given in part payment of a labourer's wage and how a few unscrupulous employers added water to this cider, keeping the unadulterated cider for themselves.

Farmers who only made small quantities of cider for themselves would often crush the apples with heavy baulks of timber before pressing. Others who made larger quantities used a stone mill operated by a horse, wearing blinkers to stop it from getting giddy as it went round and round. Later a crusher was introduced that could be driven by belts from a farmer's tractor. Many of these are still in use today and even this season we saw one working in the village.

Cider apples must have been more plentiful in the "olden" days than they are today, many orchards having been destroyed. We were told quite often a farmer would make ten "cheeses" a year, each producing a hogshead (110 gallons) of cider. The juice was often allowed to run into a trough overnight and that does surprise me.

I understand attempts were made to distill some of the cider to make apple brandy, but we never did find out whether it was successful or not. Much laughter at that stage made us realize there must have been family jokes passed down from father to son.

The old joke about putting rats in the cider to give it body is of course not true, although several farmers told me they remember their fathers or grandfathers putting in a piece of raw beef.

I am fascinated by the rhymes, verses and songs connected with cider, many of which I must admit are not very complimentary. Below are a few of my favourites.

"But hard cider as much as you please
Loose your teeth and bow your knees,
Sour your gut and make you wheeze
Thin your blood and kill your fleas,
Hard cider as much as you please"

"There was an old man and he had an old cow
and how for to keep her
He didn't quite know how,
So he built up a barn to keep his cow warm
and a drop or two of cider will do us no harm"

"Give I a gallon of cider
I like it much better than beer
Give I a gallon of cider
and you'll never give way to despair
If you're down in the dumps or unhappy
It's the drink to drive away care
So I'll give you a gallon of cider
and you'll never give way to despair"

"An orchard fair to please,
And pleasure for your mind sir,
You'd have – then plant of trees,
The goodliest you can find, sir."

"Oh the jovial days
When the apple trees do bear,
We'll drink and we'll be merry,
All the gladsome year."

"Hail to thee, old apple tree
Stand fast prop, bear well crop,
Pray God send us a howling cup
Every twig, apple big,
Every bough, apples now.

"This parish wherein cider is plentiful
hath and doth afford many people that have
and do enjoy the blessing of long life, neither
are the aged here bedridden as elsewhere, but
for the most part lively and vigorous"

"Apples now, hats full, caps full, three bushel
bags full, tallers-ole full, barns floor full"

CHAPTER 2

Commercial Cidermaking

I was recently introduced to Mr. Perry, a well known West Country cider maker. The work and bustle of his efficient cider mill was fascinating to watch. Pressing begins in the middle of October and the mill is capable of producing 2,000 gallons of cider daily. It is situated in the delightful village of Dowlish Wake in Somerset, with its thatched cottages, beautiful old church, and winding lanes.

The first thing that caught my eye was the number of large barrels (or, more correctly, pipes) which hold 120 gallons of cider. These were lying on their sides, the bung hole uppermost and chocked each side to prevent movement. Many had already been filled and round some of the bung holes one could see the white froth from the fermenting juice.

On a raised loading bank were piled large quantities of apples of all types in sacks ready to be barrowed to the conveyor. The first process was the crushing of the apples. Sacks of apples of all types and sizes were emptied into a large wooden box which fed them on to a continuously moving conveyor belt. This carried them up to a crusher where they were reduced to a pulp. The pulp was poured down into a chute which had a shutter in its base to control the flow and a trolley with a large shallow tray was positioned under the base of the chute. A wooden frame in the tray was covered by coarse polyester material. The chute was lowered, and the shutter opened momentarily to allow the correct amount of pulp to fall on to the cloth inside the frame. The sides of the cloth were then folded over to the centre, the wooden frame removed and a slatted flat pressing board was placed over the enclosed pulp, which from then on

An old press still in use. (Photo courtesy Bulmers Ltd., Hereford)

became the "Cheese". This process continued until the layers of cheeses and boards were sufficiently high to fill the hydraulic press. The trolley was then wheeled under the platen of the press and the hydraulic pump switched on. As the pressure increased the juice flowed out from between the pressing boards and was caught in the tray below. A suction hose transferred the juice direct to the waiting barrels outside.

Fermentation starts very rapidly and after the initial fermentation the cider is racked into another barrel to finish fermenting. No yeast is used in the making of this cider, which can be ready to drink in four months, and after fermentation has finished it is blended into

A modern hydraulic press extracting the juice. *(Photo courtesy Bulmers Ltd., Hereford)*

three groups, dry, medium and sweet. Vintage cider, which is left to mature for twelve months, is beautifully smooth to the palate, as we found out when we sampled it. Superb!

The method used in the following paragraph was given to me by a farmer who makes small quantities of cider in true country style, as his father did before him. After the apples are picked and left for a week they are tipped into a queer looking machine called a "scratcher" which crushes them, and they are then pressed. A sheet of sisal or hessian is placed on the bottom of a trough, then a layer of the crushed pomace or pulp, popularly called "pommy". This layer is usually four or five inches deep. The hessian is then folded over on all sides, completely enclosing the pomace. Another sheet of hessian with more pommy is placed on top and this layering is continued until the trough is filled. The press is pulled down by hand, with a pawl and ratchet preventing the screw from unwinding. After standing until the juice has ceased to run, it is then pulled down again and again until the pulp is a solid with no more juice flowing. The juice flows from the press into a wooden trough, and from there into a barrel, which is placed on its side with the bung removed. Fermentation starts after a day or two and continues for several weeks, during which time the barrel is topped up with more cider. When fermentation is finished, the bung is replaced and the cider left to mature for five or six months. The pulp from the press is either fed to the cattle, or used for feeding pheasants. Many a bird has been enticed on to a farmer's field in this way, to end up in the pot. The residue from my cider ends up on the compost heap; nothing is wasted.

In the last decade, I am told, cider drinking has been increasing up to 10 per cent annually in many areas. This is not surprising when one considers it is now possible to buy and make so many different types, and that some of the superb dry cider we now drink is quite often preferred to white wine. Obviously the fact that the price is much lower than that of wine may account for this, but I am convinced that one of the reasons why we now drink a lot of cider is because of the large range of ciders now available. Dry cider is ideal to drink with a meal and the sweeter ciders are most suitable for social drinking. One has only to visit the local off licence or store to find one can buy cider for all occasions. Commercial cider is made under the most hygienic conditions and unlike the local cidermakers' custom apples used are washed before pressing. A combination of ancient and modern methods helps to produce at one well known cider mill sufficient cider to fill almost a hundred vats, containing from 1,000 to 48,000 gallons of cider.

When ready it is eventually bottled at a rate of 12,000 bottles an hour, using the most modern equipment. A very important man in any cider establishment is the blender, who takes such pride in producing first rate cider. It is quite possible that four or five different types of cider have to be blended before he is satisfied with the final result.

Quite a lot of apples are imported from abroad, especially France, but it does appear that old orchards are being replaced and farmers encouraged to plant more cider apple trees, the names of which appear in the next chapter.

Having written about the past history of cider making and how farm cider is produced commercially, a little information on modern large scale commercial cider making may prove interesting to readers. I am indebted to Bulmers of Hereford for the information they have given to me and for allowing me to quote from it.

"The history of Bulmers began in 1887, when Mr. H. P. (Percy) Bulmer, younger son of the Rector of Credenhill, first pressed

Storing the apples at the mill. *(Photo courtesy Bulmers Ltd., Hereford)*

apples from his father's orchard. In 1888 Percy rented a warehouse in Mayford Street, Hereford, bought apples from local farmers, and made 4,000 gallons of cider. In the following year the business expanded and moved to Ryelands Street, where he was joined by his brother Fred, who became responsible for sales. The Royal Warrant was granted to the company in 1911 and has been proudly held ever since. Today Bulmers have the largest apple pressing mill in the world, and seven bottling lines, one capable of filling 14,000 flagons an hour. The annual United Kingdom cider market is well in excess of 70 million gallons, and about half of this demand is met by Bulmers with a comprehensive range of cider to suit all tastes.

Modern storage tanks for cider. *(Photo courtesy Bulmers Ltd., Hereford)*

Modern production of consistently high quality cider, backed by creative marketing and promotion techniques, has helped to turn what was once a cottage industry into a large and efficient cider-making concern.

"The season for Bulmers cider-making begins in mid-September and then builds up to a peak in October and November. The ripe apples are shaken from the trees and gathered into lorries, trucks and trailers for immediate delivery to the cider mill. The apples are tipped into silos, along which runs streams of water which wash and carry the apples into the mill. After passing through a rotary drum for a final wash, the apples are milled to a pulp and the juice is extracted by hydraulic presses. The juice is taken immediately to settling vats, before being pumped to other vats for fermentation; during fermentation the sugar in the juice is converted to alcohol. In the early years Bulmers cider was kept in 100 gallon oak casks; by 1904, 10,000 gallon vats were built, followed later by 50,000 and 60,000 gallon vats of solid English oak. Owing to a shortage of seasoned oak after World War I, the first glass-lined rectangular tanks were built in 1919 to hold 100,000 gallons. In 1954, the first steel storage tank was built – 45 ft high and 56 ft in diameter – to hold 500,000 gallons, and in 1975, a 1.6 million gallon tank named 'Strongbow' (the largest container for alcoholic liquid in the world) was built. Some 15 million gallons of cider are stored at Hereford in over 150 vats, each of which, by tradition, has its own name – Pluto, Mars, Venus, Asia, Australia, Wren, Robin or the names of those associated with the founding days of the company."

I was interested to learn that approximately 36 per cent of all adults in the country drink cider, 53 per cent being men and 47 per cent women. This is a heartening fact, because cider was renowned for its medicinal powers. In 1664 John Evelyn wrote "Generally all strong and pleasant cider excites and cleanses the stomach, strengthens Digestion and infallibly frees the Kidneys and Bladder from breeding the Gravel Stone." We are also told that Captain Cook carried cider on his ships to act as a scurvy preventative. Quite a reputation!

CHAPTER 3

Types of Apple Used

The quality of home-produced cider depends very much upon the type of apples used. Ideally, true cider apples make the best cider, but as it is not always possible for the amateur to obtain these, extra care should be taken in trying to find the correct balance of apples necessary for making cider.

Opinions do vary slightly on what makes a correct balance, but providing one has a proportion of sweet, bitter sweet and sharp apples, usually one third of each, it is possible to make a really excellent cider. We have also found that a mixture of two parts sharp to one of bitter sweet and one of sweet will produce a satisfactory brew. In Chapter 6 I have given recipes we have used and it will be noticed that in addition to the name of the apples, I have included the type, to help readers who have to make their cider with unknown varieties of apple.

The type of soil in which apples are grown can affect the sugar content and I have been told that years ago farmers would exchange some of their own crop with neighbours, even though the apples exchanged were the same variety.

Apples should be fully ripe; windfalls are excellent. After picking they should be kept for a week or two so that the skins soften, making them easier to crush. Commercial cidermakers in this area do not wash their apples, but as we are winemakers and in the habit of sterilizing all our fruits, I must admit that I do wash our apples and even cut out any diseased parts, much to the amusement of our farmer friends. I therefore leave it to the individual to decide whether or not to wash the fruit.

Gathering fruit in an ageing Herefordshire orchard in about 1908.
The decrepit trees are typical of many local orchards of the time,
ruined by three-quarters of a century of neglect.
(Photo courtesy Museum of Cider, Hereford)

Although most of the apples we have to use are unidentified varieties there are times when we are able to obtain well known varieties and we have found a mixture of the following types has always produced a satisfactory cider.

Tom Putts	A particularly good apple, medium sized, with yellow skin streaked with red. The flesh is greenish white, juicy and acid.
Cox's Orange Pippin	Sweet, very juicy, with yellow flesh.
Quarrenden	Sweet, with bright red skins. Fruits early.
James Grieve	Sweet, with yellow flesh.
Yarlington Mill	Bitter sweet, high in tannin, low in acid.
Kingston Blacks **Bloody Butcher** }	Both good for making cider.
John Downie	Small red skinned crab apple. Specific gravity of juice when tested was 1055 and the acid content 6 parts per thousand, sulphuric.

20

Bramley Seedlings are not really suitable for cider and many people avoid using them as they are so high in acid. I have found, however, that if the majority of apples are very sweet a small quantity of these can be added. When talking to farmers who made cider many years ago they remember names of apples almost unheard of today. These include Sweet Acme, Improved Pound, and Bewley Down Pippin. Morgan's Sweet, we are told, helped to make a good cider but we have not been fortunate enough to obtain any of these. I was given some interesting information by Dr. Beech, head of the cider and fruit juice section at Long Ashton Research Station, regarding the types of trees now available for cider making.

If any readers are thinking of growing apples suitable for cider, below is a list of names to consider.

Mechanical harvesting
of the cider apple crop.
*(Photo courtesy
Bulmers Ltd., Hereford)*

21

Tramlett's Bitter	
Dabinette	
Brown Snout	
Harry Master's Jersey	
Yarlington Mill	All these are bitter sweet, high in tannin, low in acid.
Fillbarrel	
Somerset Red	
Improved Dove	
Chisel Jersey	

Browns Apple	
Porters Perfection	Bitter sharp; high acid and tannin.

Sweet Coppin	Sweet, low acid and tannin.

In most of my previous recipes I have recommended readers to add a quantity of cider apples in each batch of cider they make for the best results, and if these were always easy to obtain I would continue to advise this method. In 1977, however, owing to bad weather conditions throughout the year, apples were very scarce indeed and cider apples practically non existent. Because of this I was unable to make my normal quantity of cider as the only apples available were those usually kept for culinary and cooking purposes. I was fairly fortunate to be able to buy a large quantity of small Cox's Orange and a similar amount of Crispins, a crisp medium sweet and very juicy apple. Although they were really too good for making cider I decided to use them for that purpose. Using the Walker Desmond Pulpmaster and Press, I extracted the juice to make a modest few gallons, blending the two, after testing for the sugar, acid and tannin content. This preliminary testing of the juice I have found to be absolutely essential when making cider from non-cider apples.

It is the tannin which gives cider the astringency necessary for it to be well balanced, with sufficient "bite". The Cox's Orange appeared to lack this so I decided to add a little grape tannin to correct it. The acid content was fairly high so no acid was added. I have been quite surprised on many occasions when testing the acid content of dessert apples. Contrary to popular belief, they do have a high acid content, and if fermented out to dryness the resultant cider could taste far too acid for many people. When the finished cider was sampled the result was very good indeed, which once again proved to me that it is possible to make a very good cider without using cider apples.

I have given more details of the quantities used for this particular brew in the appropriate recipe, and my advice to people with a glut of apples in their gardens is to experiment with them until eventually they will produce cider to suit their own palate. If sufficient apples are not available readers who would like to try their hand at making cider should not hesitate to make it from cider concentrates, which are normally supplied in 2 gallon cans and are as easy to use as pack beer. Although full instructions are on every can I have included the recipe to show how simple it is.

CHAPTER 4

What You Will Need

Although local cider makers, who make thousands of gallons in the season, use mechanical crushers and hydraulic presses for extracting the juice, someone who wishes to make just one or two gallons need not be deterred by any lack of such gear. There are several pieces of equipment available to the amateur cider maker and we have used most of them to produce what our friends call a very good cider.

First, there is the humble domestic mincer, either hand or electric. A No. 2 cutter should be used and it will be necessary to quarter the apples before putting them through the mincer; a large plastic bag can be placed over the nozzle to avoid losing any juice. The resultant pulp is strained through a nylon sieve into a strong nylon bag and squeezed into a plastic bucket similar to that used for winemaking.

A Walker Desmond Pulpmaster is a most useful piece of equipment, as it employs an ordinary electric drill. The two gallon container is 10 inches deep and made from high density polyethylene, the spindle and rod are plated and the sealing disc is coated with a white epoxy resin. To use it the spindle is fitted into the drill like an ordinary bit. The container is placed on the floor and the left hand held firmly on the top plate covering the apples, and the drill switched on. The whisking blade on the end of the spindle quickly reduces the apples to a slurry. We have found that cutting up the apples makes this job even easier and once they are pulped they are strained through a nylon sieve into a strong nylon bag and squeezed into a plastic bucket.

The Pulpmaster uses a two-gallon size bucket and the blade spindle slides up and down.

Any conventional electric drill can be used to power the Pulpmaster and a full load is pulped in 10 seconds.

A press is another useful item for cidermaking, especially if making 5 or 10 gallons at a time, but even if a press is used the apples must be pulped first and placed in a strong nylon bag or between layers of hessian, the ends of which must be folded over, completely enclosing the pulp to make a cheese.

A press I have found quick and simple to use is the Walker Desmond wine press. Its neat appearance immediately catches the eye, but it is when large quantities of pulverised apples and fruits are pressed one realises the efficiency of this press. A filter bag is supplied and this is placed inside the cylinder. Fruit to be pressed is put into the filter bag, the ends of which are folded over. The piston is then placed upon it and pressure is applied by rotation of a threaded rod. A steady flow of juice then flows into a shallow plastic container and from there into the gallon jars. A splash protector supplied with the press ensures that this simple operation is carried out with no mess. The whole press is easy to clean and maintain in a hygienic condition and is strongly constructed. The capacity is 4½ litres and it is 12 inches high and 4½ inches in diameter.

25

The pulp is placed in a nylon filter bag ready for pressing in either a home-made or commercially available press.

The Walker Desmond wine press makes use of nylon coating to prevent metal-to-juice contact. Piston is tested to over a ton.

A piece of equipment we have used many times is a Kenwood Juice Extractor attached to a Chef mixer. This removes the pulp and extracts the juice in one operation. The apples must be cut before being placed in the machine and the cage inside the extractor should be cleaned frequently otherwise the pulp has a tendency to drip through the outlet, so this must be watched carefully. This method is ideal for small quantities as it does take longer than pulping and pressing, but the extracted juice is free from any solid matter and therefore clears quickly. In addition to the above mentioned items which I have used, there are other pieces of equipment which I am told are extremely efficient and, purpose-made of course, other automatic mincers, shredders or pulpers, such as the hand-held BAMIX, can also be used. At the end of this chapter there are full instructions for making a simple fruit press suitable for apples, or any fruit used in winemaking.

The other requirements for cidermaking are a plastic bucket, nylon sieve, a strong nylon bag or large pieces of hessian, gallon jars, air locks and siphon, and true cider or beer bottles, with appropriate stoppers. I also recommend using a hydrometer and trial jar and an acid testing kit, although cider can be made without them. It is most essential that only true cider or beer bottles are used; ordinary wine bottles are not strong enough to hold cider, especially if it is still fermenting when bottled.

Small barrels are ideal for cidermaking. I have never used them myself, but one of the local farmers who makes large quantities of cider told me that, while the cider is still fermenting, the barrels should be topped up every other day due to the cider diminishing as fermentation proceeds. Once it has finished fermenting it is racked from one barrel to another and left to mature for six months.

Most of the items mentioned in this chapter are probably used for winemaking, therefore if the necessary quantities of apples are available, it is not difficult to make cider which we can drink whilst our wines are maturing.

MAKING A SIMPLE CIDER PRESS

Making a home made wine or cider press need not be complicated or expensive, providing one or two important factors are remembered. The first point to realize is that the main framework will have to withstand a tremendous amount of pressure, therefore it must be constructed solidly. Secondly, use no metal, for it is likely to contaminate any extracted juice with which it comes into contact.

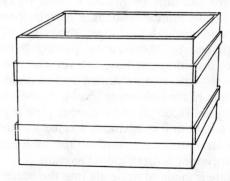

Diagram 1 A simply-constructed barrel or box, reinforced with battens.

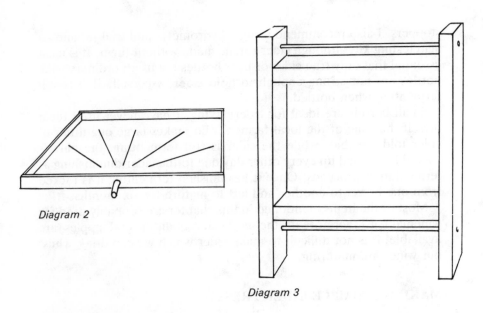

Diagram 2

Diagram 3

First, decide how large a press you require. A normal one will take a bucketful of apples (before they are pressed) so the barrel of the press will have dimensions of approximately 12"×9"×8" deep (inside dimensions). It can be constructed of solid wood, marine ply or strips of wood that are joined in the perpendicular plane, using a waterproof glue and brass screws. The barrel should be strengthened by cross battens, as in Diagram 1.

The base board can now be made. It must be large enough to stand the barrel in its middle, leaving a margin for a lipping to be glued and screwed around the edge; this adds to the strength. Further strength can be obtained by putting battens across the underneath side, providing the base is level when positioned in the frame work. A ½" hole is now drilled in the middle of the front lipping, the bottom of the hole being level with the top of the floor of the baseboard. A short length of ½" copper pipe is pushed into the hole; if it is not a tight fit it is advisable to glue it with epoxy glue. A series of ½" square battens are fixed on the base board to channel the juices to the copper outlet pipe, (Diagram 2).

A pressure plate is made to fit neatly into the barrel and should be able to move freely up and down. As this also has to withstand a lot

28

of pressure, a strong board can be built by glueing together several thicknesses of wood crossing the grain alternatively each way; this prevents warping.

Before the main framework is constructed it must be decided what method of power is to be used, whether is is to be a screw or hydraulic jack (a car jack will do). The latter is perhaps the most suitable as it saves many tedious hours of unscrewing and effort. The dimensions of the framework should allow the baseboard to sit between the pillars and have enough height for the jack to sit on top of the barrel and plunger (Diagram 3).

The frame can be constructed however you wish, provided it can stand the pressure needed. It can be of angle iron, bolted or welded together, or made from wood. The wood for a press this size should be approximately three inch square. The top and bottom cross pieces are notched into the side upright and a ½″ mild steel rod should go right across the frame, top and bottom if possible, to give a good solid finish to the job. A cross beam at the bottom to make the framework stand level is all that is now required to finish the construction. Two or three coats of polyurethane varnish will make it easy to clean the press after use.

My thanks are due to Mr. Hunt who allowed me to print these instructions for making this small press. Mr. Hunt and his wife Jean now own the establishment called Pippinfield Cider and Wine at Seaton. They have most up to date equipment and make excellent cider and apple wine.

CLEANSING

It should go without emphasis that cleanliness is an essential to all the processes involved. Although it should never be added to the cider, Chempro SDP is highly recommended as an ideal combination cleanser/steriliser which kills bacteria and is an excellent inhibitor. One main advantage is its quick action. It also has the additional ability to deodorise, so removing the chlorinated smell of other cleansers.

I use this for cleaning air-locks, bottles, jars, syphons and other equipment. Full instructions will be found on the packets and should be followed closely.

CHAPTER 5

Cidermaking Techniques

As already explained, cider is made from fermented apple juice, extracted from certain blends of apples (see Chapter 3). During fermentation, alcohol is produced by the action of the yeast from the skin of the fruit acting on the natural sugar of the fruit.

The process finishes when all the sugar has been used, with the dead yeast and any solids from the fruit forming a sediment on the bottom of the container, and the juice must be "racked" from this at least twice, both during and after fermentation. The cider may not have a very high alcoholic content.

The majority of us may not be able to obtain sufficient quantities of the particular types of apples required for a well balanced cider. On most occasions, the apples we have to use are of mixed unidentified varieties, and it was for this reason we decided to use a hydrometer to test the specific gravity of the extracted juice, and an acid testing kit for titration.

We bought several bottles of cider, both English and French, and tested them for sugar and acid content. The specific gravity of bottled commercial cider varied from 1002 to 1030, and the acid contents ranged from 3.25 to 6.0 parts per thousand (as sulphuric).

Most of the bottled cider we tried was carbonated, but we try to produce a natural sparkle by allowing the cider to produce its own carbonic gas through finishing the fermentation after it has been bottled.

After extracting the juice (see Chapter 4) we use the hydrometer to test the specific gravity and if it is below 1055 we add sufficient sugar to raise it to this level, remembering that 2½ oz of sugar will raise the gravity of 1 gallon of juice by approximately 5 degrees.

The sugar can either be dissolved in a small quantity of juice and then added to the bulk, or if caster sugar is used it can be stirred in, when it will quickly dissolve.

After this we test the acidity by using a wine testing kit. There are several different types of acidity kit available and each one carries full instructions which should be followed carefully.

Rather than give a general description of titration, I feel that it is probably wiser and easier to advise you to follow the instructions on your particular kit to make this interesting test. I have found that the amount of acid found in different types of apples varies considerably. On one occasions some juice contained 9 parts per thousand sulphuric which would have made a very sharp cider had it remained at that level.

We find that the acidity needs to be between 4 and 5 parts per thousand to produce a cider to suit our palate. On the other hand, if too many sweet, low-acid apples are used the finished cider can have a medicinal flavour. One particular batch of apples produced juice containing only 3 parts per thousand acid, so although the principal acid in cider is malic acid I added ⅜ of an ounce of mixed malic and citric acid crystals per gallon, thus raising acidity to approximately 4½ parts per thousand.

As I have already mentioned, one of our brews had 9 parts per thousand sulphuric, so we decided to use ½ oz of precipitated chalk to each gallon of juice, thus reducing the acidity by approximately 3½ parts per thousand. The precipitated chalk was mixed with about ½ pint of juice and then added to the bulk. This immediately fizzed and turned cloudy and milky looking, but it soon settled down and after two days it started to clear, with the chalk sinking to the bottom of the container. Because we used chalk this brew was racked a week later, and we were very careful to draw no sediment up from the bottom.

Although I do not think it is absolutely essential, I often add a teaspoonful of Pectolase to each gallon of juice, because in the initial stages cider looks as if it will never clear. For several years we continued to use Pectolase until there was an occasion when unintentionally it was omitted, but the cider was as brilliant as previous brews, which proved that it was not entirely necessary. Since then we have found it makes little difference whether Pectolase is used for cider, and this is why some of our more recent brews are made without it.

Yeast is not normally used in the production of cider when made in large quantities, but I was told by one farmer that if at any time his cider is slow to start he adds a little yeast "on a piece of toast" (in true old country style!) to hurry things along. We decided one year when a particular brew was slow to start fermenting that we would use a wine yeast to see if it made any appreciable difference to the finished product. After extracting the gallon of juice it was poured into one of our plastic buckets we use for winemaking and two level teaspoons of CWE 67 yeast compound stirred into it. Previous to this we had taken the specific gravity (1056) and the acidity (4 parts per thousand). The bucket was covered closely with a tight-fitting lid and placed in the warm kitchen, and that same evening it started fermenting slightly.

The following day it was fermenting vigorously, so it was transferred to a gallon demijohn and fitted with an airlock containing a little metabisulphite. Quite a large air space was left at the top of the jar for the first few days to avoid it overflowing into the airlock, but as it quietened down we gradually topped it up until we had a full gallon. We have since used several different yeasts,

Washing the apples
before crushing.

Ready to mill.

including Kitzinger, Hock, Champagne and General Purpose and all have given good results.

When yeast is added the gravity drops very quickly and there appears to be more sediment on the bottom of the jar (necessitating more frequent racking) than when only the natural yeast is employed. The finished product was also paler in colour, more like an apple wine instead of the rich golden colour associated with cider. There is a tendency for these brews to continue fermenting after the desired gravity has been reached, and to prevent it from becoming too dry a Campden tablet has to be used, resulting in cider which has no briskness. I do not object to this for occasional brews as I use cider for cooking both savoury and sweet dishes.

Unlike wine, cider does not require a hot cupboard for fermenting. A warm kitchen with a temperature around 65 degrees is ideal. I have seen cider being pumped into large barrels and left outside in the open to ferment, much to my surprise. The time taken for cider to finish fermenting can vary enormously. Some of our brews have finished in 3 weeks, whilst others continue slowly for 2 months. When the cider is ready, which means the gravity has dropped to required dryness, we bottle some of it in true cider or beer bottles, adding a teaspoonful of sugar to each quart bottle, or half a teaspoon to each pint bottle.

I must emphasize here that only true cider or beer bottles must be used: ordinary wine bottles are not strong enough to withstand

A bench model crown corker, adjustable for all bottle sizes and with a long handle for easy action.

internal pressure which may occur through fermentation finishing in the bottle.

Although we use quart beer bottles for most of our cider, I do realise they are now quite difficult to obtain. We recently tried out some of our pint beer bottles fitted with crown caps. These proved quite efficient and were useful for the odd occasion when a pint of cider was sufficient.

When bottling use a siphon for transferring from the fermentation container, making sure the outlet end of the siphon is at the bottom of the receiving bottle and so avoiding too much aeration. Old fashioned beer bottles have screw stoppers with rubber rings which are excellent, but we have used plastic snap closures or metal crown closures for which a special crimper has to be used. Both of the latter items can be obtained from stores selling winemaking equipment.

There are times when we store our cider in 5 gallon ex-sherry containers. After several weeks, when the fermentation has finished, we rack from one container into another, remove the airlock from the screw cap and replace with the original plastic tap. The container is then placed on its side on a stand in a cool place and the cider drawn off direct into the glass or jug, making excellent draught cider. This reduces any pressure that may build up, and as the bulk decreases the container will gradually collapse from the vacuum. Any slight sediment which forms will settle under the level of the tap so that the cider will remain clear to the last few glasses. Cider stored in this manner must obviously be stable, since the container will not withstand internal pressure.

Cider is normally low in alcohol as the initial starting gravity is usually between 1040 and 1060. I have never yet recorded anything higher than the latter and because we drink this in tumblers instead of wine glasses I do not think it should be made stronger. The reason why cider is reputed to put people "under the table", I think, is due to the amount one drinks, and not its strength. The following table gives the likely alcohol content of ciders made at home.

S.G.	Potential % alcohol by volume
1035	4.4
1040	5.1
1045	5.8
1050	6.5
1055	7.2
1060	7.8

This year I tried a few experiments, blending cider with white wine, and found that some of the combinations were most successful, especially when I used flower wines with a fairly pronounced bouquet. I will not say they tasted like champagne but they certainly made a very pleasant summer and social drink. I have listed below those I preferred:

Sweet elderflower and raisin (S.G. 1020) blended with dry cider.
Sweet Quince (S.G. 1015) blended with dry cider.

For both these blends I used half wine and half cider prior to drinking.

35

Siphoning into strong bottles

"... will gradually collapse from the vacuum ..."

Dry Gooseberry (S.G. 998) blended with sweet cider, using one third cider.

Dry Apple wine blended with a slightly sparkling sweet cider was exceptionally good. The specific gravity of the apple wine was 1000.

In addition to blending our cider with white wine I have on many occasions used different red wines with quite pleasing results, especially if the wine has distinct fruity flavour. I have listed those I found particularly good. The quantities often varied so I suggest trying out the combination in small quantities until the blend is satisfactory.

Sweet Autumn Fruit wine (1010) blended with dry cider. Served warm.

Dry Elderberry wine (998) mixed with dry cider plus a little sugar. Served warm.

Sweet Blackcurrant (1008) mixed with dry cider. Served chilled.

Sweet Redcurrant wine (1016) mixed with dry cider. Served chilled.

Sweet Redcurrant wine (1016) mixed with sparkling cider. Served chilled.

Sweet Blackcurrant wine, mixed with dry cider, a few cloves and a spot of cinnamon, served hot with a tot of brandy added, will frighten off any cold.

An ice cube added to each of the chilled drinks made it look very attractive.

CHAPTER 6

Possible Faults in Cider Making

There are a few faults or problems the amateur cider maker may encounter when making cider for the first time, one of the commonest being *Acetification*. The reason for this is that too much air has been allowed to reach the cider, causing the acetic bacteria to turn the alcohol into vinegar. Bad storage is one of the causes, therefore it is essential that containers are kept topped up at all times. Once the first rapid ferment has settled down, keep fermentation jars full and insert airlocks containing a little metabisulphite. In the initial stages the yeasty scum covering the surface will prevent the air coming into contact with the juice.

Darkening of the juice can occur, due in most cases to oxidation, and one way to avoid this is to add one Campden tablet to each gallon of juice as it is pressed. Over-ripe or rotten fruit could have the same effect, therefore discard any fruit that is severely blackened and mouldy as both these could cause the cider to have unpleasant flavours in addition to the enzymic darkening.

Film Yeasts can develop on a weak, low-acid, still cider if it is exposed to the air, and the first indication of this is a grey powdery film that develops on the surface. If left unchecked it will eventually turn the cider to carbon dioxide and water. There is a remedy if it is caught in its early stage. Remove as much of the film as possible then filter it into another jar using a very fine piece of linen or filter papers. Add a Campden tablet (crushed) to the gallon of cider and make sure the jar is filled to the top to exclude air.

Slow Fermentation can cause a few anxious moments for people who are making cider for the first time. Apple juice usually takes two or three days to start fermenting, but if a Campden tablet has been added to each gallon one need not be unduly worried. It may mean the conditions are not right, and the removal of the jars to a warmer place may start it fermenting. If on the other hand it refuses to ferment after a week a little wine yeast will do the trick. A slow fermentation is useful if a sweet cider is preferred as the yeast stays on the bottom of the jar, making it easy to rack, and if this is done when the gravity reaches approximately 1025 fermentation will be slowed down, eventually producing a sweet cider.

Fast Fermentation is more difficult to control and using the hydrometer at regular intervals is essential if a medium sweet cider is preferred. From our own experience we have found a fast fermentation usually produces a dry cider, as it very quickly reaches a gravity reading of 1005.

Acidity should not present any problems providing the juice is tested by taste or titration before fermentation. However, if this was not done the finished cider may not be entirely to one's liking. If it tastes flat and insipid it may mean the acid content was too low at the start. To remedy this simply mix a teaspoon of citric acid with a little of the cider then add it to the gallon. Repeat if necessary. Should the acid content be too high, add a little acid reducing compound (potassium carbonate) according to maker's instructions.

Cider storage.

Dry cider may not suit all tastes, to sweeten add a little caster sugar prior to drinking. One or two saccharin tablets per quart bottle may be added instead of sugar if preferred. They are tasteless, and there is no risk of re-fermentation.

Bottling too early can present problems and because of this, cider should be racked several times before this operation. It should be clear, with no sediment on the bottom of the jars or containers. If it is not racked sufficiently before being transferred to bottles it may result in sediment forming at the bottom of each bottle. Consequently when the bottle is opened the sediment may rise to the surface of the cider, making it cloudy and undrinkable. If this does occur, pour it immediately into another bottle, using a straining cloth, add half a teaspoon of sugar and restopper securely. After a few days it will gradually start to clear. Two more minor faults can arise through carelessness. It has already been mentioned several times in this book that true cider or beer bottles only must be used to avoid accidents, and as many of these have screw stoppers, do make sure the rubber rings are perfect and not perished. If there is any doubt, buy new ones. The other fault lies in not screwing the stoppers down sufficiently, if they are loose, air will reach the cider, causing it to oxidise and eventually turn to vinegar.

CHAPTER 7

Cider Recipes

ONE GALLON CIDER
(using additional acids)

18 lb (8.170 kilos) sweet windfalls (unknown variety)
Level teaspoon citric acid
Initial specific gravity of juice 1055

Extracted juice and strained into a gallon jar fitted with an airlock. This was kept in a warm kitchen where it started to ferment, slowly at first, but reaching a fairly vigorous fermentation after a week. By this time it had thrown such a heavy deposit we racked it into a fresh container and left it for a further two weeks. Although this cider was still fermenting, the gravity was not dropping as quickly as we expected and after racking once more we left it for 5 weeks. When we tested the gravity again we found that in 2 months it had only reached a gravity of 1035. We tasted it and found it was bland and lacked a bite, so we stirred in a level teaspoon of citric acid, racked it yet again and transferred it to the cold winery and hoped for the best.

Two months later when we checked the gravity it had dropped to 1005 much to our delight, so it was siphoned into true cider bottles and fitted with plastic closures. We added a level teaspoon of sugar to each quart bottle before filling them and made sure we left an air space of at least 2 inches at the top. This was one of our early recipes made before we started using an acid testing kit.

SPARKLING DRY
One Gallon (using Champagne yeast tablet)

10 lb (4½ kilos) Tom Putts (sharp)
5 lb (2¼ kilos) crabapples (bitter sweet)
5 lb (2¼ kilos) James Grieve (sweet)
Champagne yeast tablet
Teaspoon (5 mls) of liquid Pectolase
Campden tablet
Teaspoon (5 mls) granulated sugar

Extract the juice, take out 4 fl oz and pour into a small bottle, adding a crushed champagne yeast tablet and a teaspoon of sugar. Place the bottle in a basin containing some hot water and when the contents of the bottle are lukewarm, take it out and place in a warm cupboard for 2 days to start fermenting (this is your starter bottle).

Add a crushed Campden tablet to the juice and leave 48 hours. Test the specific gravity and if it is below 1050 add sufficient sugar to raise it to that level, remembering that 2½ oz of sugar will raise the gravity of 1 gallon of juice by approximately 5 degrees. Add Pectolase and fermenting yeast to the juice, pour it into a gallon jar and fit an airlock, filled with a little metabisulphite. Keep in a warm kitchen, not a hot cupboard; 60°F is quite sufficient. After 2 weeks when a sediment will have formed at the bottom of the jar, rack into a fresh container and test the specific gravity, which by now should read between 1010 and 1015. (Do not allow the gravity to drop below 1005 unless a very dry cider is preferred). Siphon off into a fresh container, still fitted with an airlock and put it in a cool place for two more weeks, testing the gravity occasionally until it reaches 1005 or just over. The cider is now ready to bottle. Using a siphon carefully, bottle in true cider or beer bottles, priming them with a level teaspoonful of sugar to each quart.

Make sure a space is left at the top of at least 2 inches. Fit plastic snap closures or metal crown closures, applied with a proper crimping tool.

ONE GALLON DRY STILL CIDER

10 lb (4½ kilos) Tom Putts (sharp)
5 lb (2¼ kilos) crabapples (bitter sweet)
5 lb (2¼ kilos) Charles Ross (sweet)
Graves yeast tablet
Campden tablet
Teaspoons (5 mls) liquid Pectolase

Use the method described for 1 gallon of sparkling cider and continue the fermentation until the gravity reaches 1005, or just a little above. At this stage, rack into a fresh jar, adding a crushed Campden tablet. Leave in a cool place for a further 2 weeks then bottle in true beer or cider bottles making sure the outlet end of the siphon is at the bottom of the receiving bottle and so avoid too much aeration.

5 GALLON DRY CIDER

For each gallon of cider I used approximately:
10 lb (4½ kilos) Tom Putts (sharp)
10 lb (4½ kilos) mixed dessert apples
1 teaspoon (5 mls) Pectolase
Champagne yeast tablet (made into a starter bottle with a little extracted juice and a teaspoonful of sugar)
Campden tablets (crushed)

Wash the fruit and remove any diseased part. Extract juice with equipment available, add a Campden tablet and leave 24 hours. At the same time pour about 4 oz of juice into a small bottle, adding the crushed yeast tablet and sugar, shake it well and place in a warm cupboard to start fermenting. Test the specific gravity of the juice and if below 1050 add sufficient sugar to bring it to this level, remembering that 2½ oz of sugar raises the gravity of 1 gallon juice by 5 degrees. After 2 days add Pectolase and yeast starter, then pour into a 5 gallon container fitted with an airlock containing a little metabisulphite. A sediment will form at the bottom of the container, therefore after 2 weeks rack into a fresh container and test the gravity. Continue to ferment, racking occasionally until the specific gravity reaches 1005; do not allow it to drop below this: keep a careful check. Take out half a pint of cider, add a Campden tablet, mix well, then pour it into the bulk.

I now place another 5 gallon container on a low stool in my winery or any cool place suitable for storing. When the cider reaches a gravity of 1005 I rack into this, adding a crushed Campden tablet to each gallon. If using the 5 gallon ex-sherry container replace the airlock with the original plastic tap and turn the container on its side with the tap at the base. One person will find this difficult, but two people can manage it quite easily. Leave for a week or two, then draw off a glass to reduce any pressure that may build up. One word of advice: if this method of storing is adopted, check frequently that the pressure inside the container does not build up from the ferment, causing the sides of the container to bulge slightly. If this does happen, reduce the pressure by drawing off a few glasses, and as the bulk is used the container will gradually collapse from the vacuum. Any slight sediment which forms will settle under the level of the tap so that the cider drawn off will be clear. This is a good way of storing 5 gallons if no barrel is available; one has no bottling problems.

1 GALLON CIDER
(using precipitated chalk)

Approximately 20 lb (9 kilos) apples (unknown variety, mostly culinary)
8 oz (227 grams) granulated sugar
½ oz (14 grams) precipitated chalk
Initial gravity of juice 1050

28th October. Extracted juice, strained through nylon cloth into a plastic bucket and tested the specific gravity, which was 1050. Added 4 oz sugar to raise the S.G. to approximately 1058. Stirred well and poured into a gallon jar fitted with an airlock, containing a little metabisulphite. Placed in a warm kitchen.

9th November. Tested the S.G. which was 1010. Racked into a fresh jar, being careful not to disturb the sediment at the bottom of the jar.

23rd November. Tested the S.G. and finding it 1005 degrees added another 4 oz of sugar as it tasted quite sharp. This did not make much difference to the taste so decided to test the cider for acid content and found it was 9 parts per thousand sulphuric. This was far too high to be pleasant so we decided we would experiment and reduce the acid with the aid of precipitated chalk. Mixed ½ oz. with a glass of cider and stirred it into the bulk. It immediately foamed and fizzed and turned quite cloudy and milky looking. After a week it had dropped a heavy deposit on the bottom of the jar so it was carefully racked into a fresh jar. The acidity was tested and we found it 6½ parts per thousand and much more to our liking. Removed jar to a cool place and left it for a month.

21st December. Tested the specific gravity which read 1005 (the same as it was before adding the second 4 oz sugar in November. Racked once again and left for 3 months.

20th March The cider was now brilliant so it was siphoned into quart beer bottles, adding a level teaspoon of sugar to each quart bottle. We used the screw stoppers that were supplied with the beer bottles, but we bought new rubber rings and found them ideal. Until this batch we had always been wary about using screw stoppers, but providing true beer (or cider) bottles are used it is quite safe. We still had two of these bottles a year after making and it was delightful, brilliant and smooth, with a slight briskness when poured out. We were sorry we had been in such a hurry to drink this particular cider and wished we had made 5 gallons instead of 1. This does prove, however, that testing for acidity is just as important as taking the specific gravity, if unknown varieties of apples are used.

In this particular recipe I have included the dates as noted in my record book.

1 GALLON SWEET CIDER

10 lb (4½ kilos) Cox's Orange Pippins (windfalls) (sweet)
5 lb (2¼ kilos) Tom Putts (acid)
5 lb (2¼ kilos) unknown variety (bitter sweet)
Hock yeast tablet
1 teaspoon (5 mls) Pectolase
3 Campden tablets

Prepare fruit and extract juice as described in Chapter 4. Test the gravity and if below 1060 add sufficient sugar to raise it to this level.

Add a crushed Campden tablet and leave 24 hours in a covered plastic bucket. Add a teaspoon of Pectolase and a crushed yeast tablet and transfer it to a gallon jar fitted with an airlock containing a little metabisulphite. Leave at room temperature (not in a hot cupboard) for 2 weeks when a sediment will have formed at the bottom of the jar. After adding the yeast this particular brew took 2 days before it started fermenting; be patient.

Continue to rack weekly, testing the gravity each time until it reaches 1020 or nearabouts. This gallon dropped to 1020 in four weeks. Rack into a fresh jar, adding 2 crushed Campden tablets, replace airlock and keep the jar in a cold room. If a slight sediment forms again after a further 2 weeks, rack once again. This cider was used from the jar at Christmas time for a party, and although it was only 10 weeks old it was quite good. It also makes excellent cider cup, the recipe for which I have given under that heading.

5 GALLONS CIDER
(country style)

For each gallon of cider we used 20 lb (9 kilos) of mixed unknown types of apples, some of which were said to be cider apples.

Extracted the juice using a Pulpmaster and press. Some of the apples were rather hard so after cutting them and putting them into the Pulpmaster we added about 1 pint of juice to each load and this made the task of pulping almost a hundredweight of apples quite simple. If no juice is available, water could be used for the first load. The pulp was then put into a nylon bag placed inside the press, and the juice extracted into a plastic bucket. The gravity of this juice was 1055 so it was left at that and poured into a 5 gallon ex-sherry container. We kept this in the warm kitchen overnight and next evening we were surprised to see it fermenting well. After 5 days the gravity was 1032, and after 12 days it was down to 1010. It was then racked into a fresh container and removed to the cold winery. We left this brew undisturbed for a month and when it was tested the gravity had dropped to 1005. Although we had not used any yeast or sugar, there was still a slight sediment at the bottom of the container when it was racked for the second time. Four weeks later we again racked it into its storage container. We drew off a glass at Christmas time, 9 weeks after making it, to see how it was progressing and found it quite clear and stable but rather harsh, so we left it to mature till the following March, when it was very pleasant. This brew was not bottled, but left in the 5 gallon container, drawing it off when required, and it was excellent draught cider.

10 GALLONS DEVON CIDER

For each gallon of cider we used:
20 lb (9 kilos) mixed cider apples (one third sharp, bitter sweet and sweet)
1 Campden tablet

15th October. Washed apples, removed diseased parts, bruised and slightly brown apples were included. Extracted juice with a Pulpmaster and press. Strained through a nylon bag into two 5 gallon ex-sherry containers. Placed in a warm kitchen.
Specific gravity of juice 1055.
Acid content 4.75 parts per thousand sulphuric.
17th October. Fermenting well.
21st October. Fermenting furiously, had to remove airlock frequently to clean it. Tested the gravity, 1022 (a drop of 33 degrees in 6 days).
26th October. Tested gravity 1012. Fermentation slowed down considerably.
30th October. Racked into a fresh container, heavy sediment on the bottom. S.G. 1006. Added one Campden tablet to each gallon. Removed to cold winery.
9th November. S.G. 1005. Good colour and beginning to clear.
23rd November. S.G. 1005. Racked, by siphoning into a fresh container. Beautiful colour and very clear. Very slight sediment on bottom.
29th December. S.G. 1004. Racked once again and placed the container in its storage position. At this stage the cider was clean tasting, extremely good colour, clear and fairly stable. It was rough, which is to be expected at 2 months old.
We were unable to bottle all this cider, so 5 gallons was left in its storage container, to be drawn off when required. The other 5

gallons we transferred to single gallon jars, adding ½ lb of sugar to the 5 gallons of cider, and refitted the airlock, containing a little metabisulphite.

From January onward we drew off occasional glasses from the 5 gallon container, until in March we were able to raise the glass and pronounce it ready for drinking.

In February we had sufficient quart cider bottles, so decided to siphon the cider in single gallons, into the bottles, adding a teaspoonful of sugar to each quart bottle and allowing at least 2 inch head space. (I must mention again that only true cider or beer bottles must be used for bottling cider.) Plastic closures were used on this occasion.

Our first bottle we tried in April and although it did not have a great deal of sparkle it was brisk enough to be refreshing.

The finished specific gravity of these 2-5 gallons varied slightly, the 5 gallon bulk being 1002 and the bottled cider 1005.

If a sweeter cider is required sugar can be added prior to drinking. Caster sugar is ideal for this purpose as it dissolves easily.

TRADITIONAL CIDER

2 Kilos Crispins
2 kilos cider apples
3½ kilos Cox's Orange

11th November. Pulped and pressed apples. S.G. of juice 1040. Acid content 3½ ppt sulphuric. Added approximately 200 grams of sugar plus one crushed Campden tablet to each gallon of juice to raise the gravity to 1055. Poured juice into gallon jars.

13th November. Juice started to ferment.

16th November. Vigorous ferment, placed plastic bags over the necks of the jars.

26th November. Very vigorous ferment, had to clean the necks of the jars to insert air locks containing a little metabisulphite. Tested gravity which was 1008.

11th December. Fermentation slowed down considerably. Racked into clean jars, topping up with reserve cider. Tested gravity: 1004.

"You'll have to be satisfied with cider"

Added a crushed Campden tablet to each gallon, returning it to the cold winery.

This batch was racked in the following February, and again in March, prior to bottling. Ready to drink in May.

CIDER FROM COX'S AND COOKERS

4 kilos small Cox's
3½ kilos cooking apples, unknown variety } **for each gallon**
150 grams of sugar
Fermalent R yeast
1 Campden tablet
5 drops of grape tannin

11th December. Pulped and pressed apples. Tested the specific gravity and added the sugar to raise it to 1055. Tested for acid content and found it was 7 ppt sulphuric acid. Sprinkled a sachet of Fermalent R on the surface and stirred it well.

49

12th December. Slight fermentation.

14th December. Fermentation vigorous. Continued fermenting in bin, stirring occasionally.

23rd December. Racked into gallon jars and fitted airlocks, containing a little metabisulphite. Specific gravity had dropped to 1005 so added 1 Campden tablet. Placed in cold winery.

22nd January. Racked again into fresh jar as there was a small amount of sediment in the bottom of the jar.

30th March. Tested gravity: 1004. Bottled into true cider bottles adding a teaspoon of sugar into each quart bottle before siphoning in the cider.

2nd May. Sampled the first bottle. Excellent dry cider with a very slight sparkle. Good colour and bouquet.

SUPER SWEET CIDER

This particular batch of cider was such a superb sweet cider, enjoyed by so many people, I decided to include it in the book, although I will be quite frank and admit it was too sweet for my taste.

Starting gravity 1060
Acidity 4 ppt
3 gallons
8¾ lb (4 kilos) Sunset Queen
8¾ lb (½ kilos) Rev. Wilkes
18 lb (8.170 kilos) cider apples
13 lb (6 kilos) Morgan's Sweet

1st November. Using the Desmond Walker Pulpmaster and Press, extracted juice, added three Campden tablets. Used a 3 gallon bin.

4th November. Started fermenting. Stirred occasionally and kept covered.

12th November. Tested specific gravity 1026. Racked into gallon jars.

20th November. Tested gravity again, 1010. Added a Campden tablet to each gallon. Very clear, good colour and bouquet. No sparkle.

31st December. Decided we needed a sweet cider for a party, tested gravity which was still 1010. Used half a gallon for cider punch and used remaining half straight from the jar, excellent draught cider.

17th March. Bottled remaining two gallons in true cider bottles. Did not add sugar to each bottle as we normally do as the gravity was still 1010, and we wanted it to be a still cider.

8th April. Opened first bottle for Good Friday and voted it excellent for social drinking. It was also useful for blending with a particularly dry cider we had on hand.

COX'S CIDER

For one of our gallons we used approximately:
18 lb (8.170 kilos) Cox's Orange apples
20 drops of grape tannin
1 heaped teaspoon C.W.E. yeast
2 Campden tablets

Extracted juice with Kenwood Juice Extractor, added a Campden tablet. Specific gravity of juice was 1055 and although at the time we did not test for acid content we realized it was high in acid by the taste. After a week there was no sign of fermentation so we added a teaspoon of yeast and moved it to a warmer spot. Within two days there was a fermentation so it was left in the gallon jar, fitted with an air lock containing a little metabisulphite for a further two weeks. By this time fermentation was quite vigorous and a sediment was on the bottom of the jar. Racked into a fresh jar making sure I carried over a little yeast as I did not want it to stop fermenting. Four weeks later it was racked again and a gravity reading taken and we were pleased to see it was 1010. The taste however lacked a bite so we added the grape tannin in the hope that it would give the cider the astringency necessary for a well balanced cider. Two months later when it was racked again the gravity was still 1010 so a Campden tablet was added and we used this particular brew as a sweet draught cider. The tannin had made a considerable difference to the taste and we are pleased to know we can make a very drinkable cider from dessert apples.

PERRY 'N CIDER
(1 gallon)

9 lb (4.2 kilos) mixed apples: Cox's Orange, Tom Putt, James
  Greaves Cookers
5 lb (2.27 kilos) pears (Beurre Hardy used)
2 Campden tablets
1 bottle fermenting cider
Specific gravity 1052
Acidity 6 ppt sulphuric

12th October. Washed fruit, removed mouldy portions. Extracted juice using a Kenwood Juice Extractor. A Campden tablet was put into the jar before filling. Strained through nylon straining bag. The pulp from the fruit I pressed with the Desmond Walker Press to obtain the maximum amount of juice.

15th October. No sign of fermentation so I took a bottle of cider from the jar, replacing it with a bottle of fermenting cider from a previous batch. Fitted airlock containing metabisulphite.

16th October. Started fermenting.

21st October. Fermenting well. Tested specific gravity 1030. Cleaned airlock.

30th October. Rather a heavy deposit on the bottom of the jar, so it was racked and strained through straining bag. Topped up with cider from spare jar. Specific gravity 1010.

7th November. Clearing very quickly. Specific gravity 1005. Racked again for the last time, added a crushed Campden tablet and placed it in the cold winery.

14th November. Tasted a glass and was quite impressed.

SMALL CIDER

This is the name given to cider made from apple juice to which water and sugar has been added. At times this can be very useful, especially if a particular brew is high in acid as the sugar and water will help mask the acid taste. I have found making a quantity of Small Cider also useful when we have a small amount of juice left over after pressing which is not sufficient to fill the only available container.

When making this, add required amount of water and test the specific gravity adding sufficient brown sugar to raise the gravity to 1058 or thereabout, 2½ oz raising the gravity of 1 gallon juice by approximately five degrees. We added three pieces of bruised root ginger to the gallon and left it in the cider until ready to drink. Whether to add yeast is a debatable point, on several occasions the juice started fermenting after a few days so none was added whereas sometimes nothing happened and a teaspoon of CWE yeast was sprinkled in to help it "get going". My advice therefore when making Small Cider is to wait three or four days and if there is no sign of fermentation however slight add a little yeast to help it start. We have found Small Cider very good to drink, the main difference being the colour, in most cases it is much lighter and more like apple wine which is not surprising when one considers apple wine contains similar ingredients. I presume this is the reason brown sugar was used instead of white. Small Cider made without yeast is ready to drink in a matter of weeks and if made in October it can be drunk at Christmas.

MAKING CIDER USING CONCENTRATE

With the introduction of new brands of cider kits and concentrates, I feel a few words on this subject may be helpful to readers making cider for the first time. In addition to making this type of cider, as instructed on the tin, they can also be used for blending. If cider apples are not available, a tin of cider-apple concentrate added to a mixed bag of dessert and culinary apples will make quite a good drinkable cider. During the past eight years I have used many different brands of concentrates, all of which gave good results. Although manufacturers claim the cider is ready to drink in a matter of days, giving it longer to mature improves it immensely.

In this chapter I have given the instructions which are normally printed on the reverse side of the labels, showing readers how simple it is to use these cider kits. The specific gravity of the concentrates I have used was around 1044, therefore if the cider is allowed to ferment out to 1000 the alcohol content would be approximately 5½%. If a stronger cider is required extra sugar in the initial stages will raise the alcohol content. Cider with a very low starting gravity, below 1040, may not keep as well as one with a higher starting gravity.

Should a batch of cider made with non-cider apples lack the characteristic cidery taste, a tin of cider concentrate made as instructed on the tin, plus a little grape tannin and extra acid should improve it.

When I mention tins of cider concentrate I normally mean the two gallon cans. It is nice to know that even in a bad season when apples are scarce we can still make our own cider.

I recommend bottling cider. Quite often a slight fermentation continues in bottle causing the cider to be petillant when poured out. I have been told that a soda siphon can be used to give cider a sparkle, but not having used one I cannot comment.

BREWMAKER SPARKLING CIDER

Empty the contents of the can into a fermentation bin and add 340 grams (12 oz) white household sugar. Boil two pints of water, allow to cool slightly and stir into the mixture, using some of the hot water to rinse out the can. Add a further 14 pints of cold water, stir well then sprinkle the yeast (which is supplied with the cider kit) on top and fit the fermentation lid. The temperature of the liquid should be around 70°F. Place the fermentation bin in a warm room or airing cupboard to maintain this temperature as far as possible. As the cider ferments, the sugar is turned into alcohol and carbon dioxide gas is given off; the bubbles can be seen rising to the surface. Fermentation shold be finished after about 5-10 days (the bubbles will cease to rise to the surface).

Caution: Bottling before fermentation has finished can result in burst bottles or over-pressurising when a barrel is used. A Brewmaker beer hydrometer, while not essential, will give you the ideal bottling or barrelling point. Ensure the gravity reading is 1000 or less.

Bottling your cider.Put a maximum of one level teaspoon of sugar per pint into each bottle and siphon the cider from the fermentation bin into your bottles, leaving a two inch space at the top for the secondary fermentation to give your cider sparkle. Seal the bottles and keep at a warm temperature for a few days and then remove to a

The Brewmaker Kit is simple to use and widely available.

cool place for storing. Your cider is now ready for drinking but will improve if allowed 2-3 weeks to mature. When serving pour all the contents of the bottle in one go into a jug carefully so as not to disturb the sediment at the bottom of the bottle. Serve chilled.

I have included this method, which is printed on the reverse side of the label of Brewmaker Cider, to show readers how simple it is to make.

MY METHODS OF USING CIDER CONCENTRATE

1 tin Cider Concentrate (1 kg)
12½ pints cool water
14 oz (357 grams) granulated sugar
2 teaspoons citric acid
½ teaspoon grape tannin
Campden tablets
1 sachet Champagne yeast (made into a starter bottle)

Into a two gallon bin pour the can of cider concentrate plus the same quantity of hot water. Mix well then add 7 litres of cool water plus the sugar, and stir well to dissolve the sugar. Mix in the acid and tannin plus the fermenting yeast. Cover with a lid. Specific gravity of juice etc. was 1044. When fermenting pour it into 2 gallon container fitted with an airlock containing a little metabisulphite. Test the gravity at frequent intervals and when it reaches 1004 rack it into a fresh container adding a crushed Campden tablet per gallon. Fermentation will slow down considerably. The cider will now start to clear so test the gravity after about a week and when it reaches a little over 1000 siphon it into your bottles, adding a level teaspoon sugar. Leave a two inch space at the top for the secondary fermentation to give the cider a sparkle.

5 GALLONS CIDER USING UNKNOWN VARIETIES OF APPLES AND CONCENTRATE

Approximately ½ cwt (25 kilos) mixed windfall apples
1 kg tin Brewmaker Concentrate
Campden tablets
1 teaspoon grape tannin
Citric acid if necessary

Wash the fruit, crush, press and extract juice. This quantity of apples will probably produce about three gallons of juice, if not use a few more to make that quantity. Add metabisulphite equivalent to one Campden tablet per gallon and leave for two days, then siphon from the container into the fermentation bin and cover closely. Make up the concentrate as instructed on the tin, then pour it into the bin with the apple juice. Test the gravity and if below 1050 add sufficient sugar to increase it to that level, remembering that 2½ oz sugar will raise the gravity of one gallon of the juice by approximately 5 degrees. After about 5-6 days if fermenting well pour it into an ex-wine or other five gallon container and fit an airlock containing a little metabisulphite. Allow to ferment until the gravity reaches 1000, rack it into a fresh container, add the equivalent of one Campden tablet per gallon and leave it to mature three months.

INSTANT "CIDER" TYPE APPLE DRINK

1½ lb (680 grams) cooking apples (windfalls suitable)
1½ lb (680 grams) dessert apples (windfalls suitable)
1lb (454 grams) sugar
2 lemons

56

6 pints (3 litres) cold water
1 piece of bruised root ginger
6 cloves

Wash apples, remove diseased parts and put through a mincer; do not peel. Place in a plastic bucket with cloves, sugar, root ginger, grated rind from one lemon, juice from both lemons and water. Mix well together, cover closely and leave in a kitchen for a week, stirring twice daily. Strain carefully into a gallon jar (do not press the pulp too hard), fit an airlock containing a little metabisulphite and leave for another week. Using a siphon, transfer to a fresh jar or siphon into true cider bottles, fitted with plastic closures. Leave an air space of at least 2 inches.

I think it is essential to use plastic closures for this type of drink, as should it ferment too much when in bottle the stoppers will blow and there is no danger of burst bottles. Ready to drink a week after bottling, but improves with keeping.

This is not my own recipe, but I have tasted the drink, which is quite pleasant.

CIDER VINEGAR

Cider vinegar is quite expensive to buy, but quite simple to make. Place ½ lb sugar into a gallon container, add approximately 6 pints dry cider and ½ pint of good malt vinegar.

Mix well, cover with a piece of linen or clean material and tie down securely. Alternatively an airlock can be fitted provided no water is used in it.

Leave for 3 or 4 months when it will be ready to use.

This cider vinegar may be used in most salads or any recipes in which vinegar is used.

Mix with a little honey, salt and pepper to make a salad dressing. In addition to cider vinegar I also use olive oil for dressing salads. This dressing is good poured over a crisp lettuce.

Add a little to cabbage when making coleslaw.

Use in place of ordinary vinegar with freshly boiled beetroots.

Cucumber is improved if sprinkled with cider vinegar.

To make Vinaigrette I mix:
2 tablespoons olive oil
1 tablespoon cider vinegar
½ crushed clove of garlic (rubbed round bowl)
Salt and pepper
½ teaspoon caster sugar
¼ teaspoon made mustard

Mix the cider vinegar, mustard, salt and pepper. Pour oil slowly on to the vinegar, then whisk until well blended.

Use cider vinegar for making mint sauce.

To make an unusual orange salad to serve with duck: peel the orange, remove pith and skin, cut across into slices. Place on a bed of lettuce and pour over a little cider vinegar, sprinkle with a pinch of caster sugar.

1984 BREW

Collected as many apples as we were able to use and left them for ten days to soften slightly. These were a mixed bag, mostly cider apples whose names have long been forgotten, plus Newton Wonders and a few Yarlington Mill. They were washed and any really bad apples removed, fortunately these were very few. We then crushed and pressed them using the Rauch crusher and press and because it was the first time we had used them together we were pleased at the amount of juice pressed out.

Tested the specific gravity of the juice which was the highest we have ever recorded, 1058, and the acid content was 5 ppt. Tasted the juice and because it appeared to be well balanced it was not necessary to use any tannin or extra acid. Metabisulphite, equivalent to one Campden tablet or 50 ppm per gallon, had been put into the container before adding the juice. This was left 48 hours and then racked into the fermentation bin. One cannot do that for very large amounts, but when making five gallons at a time it is easy and removes much of the sediment which often settles on the bottom of the container. Fitted an airlock containing a little metabisulphite and left it in the garage. After 3 days it was fermenting and continued to do so quite vigorously. At the time of writing it had only been made

3 weeks so I cannot say how the finished product will turn out, but having tested the gravity and found it had dropped considerably I tasted it and although it was obviously rough I think this batch will be really good.

SCRUMPY

Scrumpy, the best-known name associated with cider, is made from traditional cider apples only, with no other additive. The alcohol is obtained from the working of the apples' own sugar and yeast. It is usually made in barrels and once the apples are crushed and pressed the juice is transferred to the barrels and allowed to ferment naturally. Once it starts fermenting a creamy coloured frothy scum can be seen coming from the bung hole. Although this prevents air reaching the cider, a cork is placed loosely in the hole and covered with several thicknesses of hessian. If the covering is thick enough that is often sufficient without a cork. At this first stage the barrels are kept topped up with fresh juice, when necessary.

Once fermentation ceases, which can be anything from one to three months or even longer, it is bunged down tight and left to mature. Many of the barrels used had contained rum or whisky and this was thought to give the cider extra flavour.

LARGER BATCHES

When we make our large batches of cider we use the "Rauch" crusher and press that are made for each other. The crusher is well made with a very sturdy hopper that holds approximately 10 lb of fruit. The large circular handle turns two rollers of acid-resistant cast aluminium which have revolving teeth which pull the apples downwards between the rollers, which are adjustable, so that the crushed fruit appears to be well pulped. As the crusher sits on the basket of the press, which has a removable straining bag of very strong nylon, the pulp pours through with no more handling. It is easier to use if the hopper is only half full to start, adding more apples gradually until the basket is sufficiently loaded for pressing to begin.

To accommodate the crusher being placed on the basket of the

The Rauch crusher in use; note the metal frame tilted back to allow the hopper to be positioned.

The Rauch press with the frame returned to vertical and the screw acting on the pressing boards.

press, the metal frame is tilted back and locked in position by the two feet at the base of the press. When there is sufficient pulp to be pressed, the crusher is lifted off, the frame pulled over to its original upright position and the pressing boards placed in position on the pulp prior to screwing down the press. Directly pressure is applied via the screw, juice will begin to flow, so never forget to have a suitable container ready in position. The secret of pressing, of course, is to let the juice flow, stop screwing until it almost ceases, then screw down further and repeat. A refinement on this press is the ratchet drive that is used to exert maximum pressure on the pulp, with an ingenious method of reversing the drive when releasing the pressure.

After pressing is finished, the frame is tilted back, the nylon bag containing the fairly dry pulp lifted out (it all goes on our compost heap), then the crusher is replaced resting on the basket loaded with more apples and the process repeated. If you are catching the juice

The pulp before pressing.

in a two gallon container do not forget to put sufficient metabisulphite powder in and stir the liquid round to dissolve it. This will prevent the apple juice oxidising.

When the day's crushing is finished all that is necessary to clean it is to stand the crusher on its side and play the hose pipe on it, at the same time turning the handles so that the rollers are cleaned. The press is just as easy to clean: remove cage and the base from the iron frame, hose down and allow to drain. The substantial nylon bag is turned inside out, washed thoroughly and "drip dried".

We bought the "Rauch" crusher and press from Derek S. Pearman, Loftus, 9 Oakleigh Way, Mitcham, Surrey.

CHAPTER 8

Cider Cups

2 pints (1.12 litres) sweet cider
½ lemon (sliced)
Small bottle ginger ale
2 cloves
Few slices cucumber
Mix all together in a bowl and leave for an hour. Serve very cold.

★

2 pints (1.12 litres) sweet cider
2 pints (1.12 litres) soda water
Sliced cucumber
Ice cubes
Mix all together in a bowl, add ice cubes and serve immediately.

★

2 pints (1.12 litres) medium sweet cider
Small bottle ginger ale
Small bottle soda water
Wine glass of sherry
Melon cubes
Sliced orange or lemon
Mix all together in a bowl, leave one hour and serve cold.

★

2 pints (1.12 litres) sparkling cider (dry)
1 bottle ginger ale

2 oz (57 grams) caster sugar
Slices of cucumber
Lemon slices
A few sprigs of mint

Mix cider, ale, sugar and mint in a bowl. Add cucumber and leave one hour. Serve with an ice cube and a slice of lemon in each glass.

★

2 pints
(1.12 litres) sweet sparkling cider
Small bottle soda water
Small bottle ginger ale
Any tinned or fresh fruit available

Mix all together and leave 1 hour. Serve with an ice cube in each glass.

★

MULLED CIDER CUP

4 pints (2.24 litres) sweet cider
4 cloves
Few slices of lemon or orange
Pinch of cinnamon
1 piece bruised root ginger

Place in a double saucepan, heat through and allow it to infuse ½ hour. Serve in thick heatproof glasses.

★

COLD CHASER
(taken at bed-time)

"... a chaser ... at bedtime ..."

1 glass sweet cider
Generous pinch of ground ginger

Sprinkle the ginger into a glass of cider. Almost bring it to the boil, pour a mug and drink it as hot as possible. A well known West Country remedy.

FRUIT CIDER CUP

2 pints (1.12 litres) medium dry cider
2 tablespoons sugar
½ lemon
Bottle soda water
½ orange
Slices of red unskinned apple
½ lb (227 grams) soft berry fruits (in season)
Ice cubes

Place all ingredients except ice cubes in a large basin, leave half an hour. A short while before serving add ice cubes.

CIDER SOURCES

We are indeed very fortunate in the West Country having so many establishments where cider produced on the premises can be bought. Holiday-makers could spend a most enjoyable day going round their chosen "route du cidre" admiring the countryside which often surrounds the cider mills. In addition to the very large commercial firms whose products are known nationwide, there are many local producers, especially farmers who make and sell cider to the public. Providing one does not expect to be shown around at the height of the season when most people are working flat out crushing and pressing, visitors are often welcomed. Several large firms are pleased to arrange tours for groups of people but obviously these are arranged in advance. A few have shops where all types of souvenirs can be bought. Below are the names of several cider mills or farms where I know one can buy good cider.

Brympton D'Evercy, Yeovil, Somerset. Owner Mr. Charles C. Ponsonby Fane. Beautiful country house, extensive gardens and vineyards. A museum, gift and plant shop, cider and cream teas and many other attractions combine to make a visit to Brympton a most enjoyable day out. Mr. Ponsonby Fane gave a most interesting talk to a party of our wine circle members several years ago.

Sheppy's, Three Bridges, Bradford on Tone, Taunton, Somerset. Sheppy's cider is well known in the West Country, having won many awards for real farmhouse cider. Here again there is a museum and one can buy cream and cheese to take away. Mrs. Sheppy told me that if large parties wish to be shown over the mill and farm they would like to have advance notice. Well worth a visit.

Perry Brothers Cider Mill, Orchardlands, Dowlish Wake, Somerset. Mr. Perry's cider mill was one of the first I visited when we came down to live in the West Country. When I told him how interested I was in making cider he was most helpful. There is a museum attached which holds some of the most interesting items I have seen. There is a shop selling a wide range of cider, gifts of all kinds and many other items associated with cider.

Pippinfield Cider and Wines, Harepath Hill, Seaton, Devon. Owners Mr. and Mrs. D. Hunt. Situated not far from the popular seaside resort of Seaton, Pippinfield Cider has a good reputation in this area. Until last year a beautiful old press was used but has now been replaced by modern machinery. A good place to buy your cider.

Woodcote Farm, Hawkchurch, Axminster, Devon. Owner Mr. Charles Raymond. Our local cider maker who still uses a 300-year-old cider press. Real farmhouse cider is made and sold here and it certainly packs a punch.

Burrow Hill Cider, Pass Vale Farm, Burrow Hill, Kingsbury Episcopi, Martock, Somerset. Although Martock is not far from where I live, I have not yet visited this mill, owned by Mr. Julian Temperly. A friend of mine who lives in the area praised this cider so much I had to include it in my list of recommended cider mills. Mr. Temperley's cider, I am told, has won prizes at the Royal Bath and West Show plus other worthy awards. Well worth visiting with beautiful surrounding countryside.

Heck's Farmhouse Cider, 9 & 10 Middle Leigh, Street, Somerset. Another mill recommended by the same person who gave me Mr. Temperley's address. Mr. Heck's cider has also won awards at the Royal Bath and West Show. I am told this cider is superb, especially the sweet type. If you visit this establishment, allow time to walk down Street High Street (where there are several shops selling Clarkes shoes at reasonable prices . . .)

CHAPTER 9

Cooking With Cider

SAVOURY BOILED BACON

A piece of boiling bacon approximately 2 lb (907 grams) in weight
½ pint (¼ litre) dry cider
½ pint (¼ litre) water

If the bacon appears salty, soak in warm water for an hour. Place in saucepan with cider and water. Bring slowly to the boil, removing any scum that rises. Cover with a lid and simmer very slowly for about an hour and a quarter, turning it over once during cooking. If this joint is to be served cold, allow it to remain in the cooking liquid till cold.

BRISKET OF BEEF

A piece of brisket of beef about 2lb (907 grams) in weight
1 oz. (28 grams) dripping
¼ pint (⅛ litre) of stock (cube)
Teaspoonful of flour
Salt and pepper

MARINADE
½ pint (0.14 litre) medium dry cider
1 onion, bayleaf and pepper
Place beef in above, marinate overnight

Melt dripping in saucepan, brown the beef for one minute each side. Add half the cider and a little salt. Cover with a lid, turn down the heat to as low as possible and cook for about an hour and a quarter or until tender, turning the meat occasionally. Remove from pan and keep hot. To the drippings in the pan, mix in the flour, scraping well round the sides. Pour in the stock, adjust seasoning and strain into a sauce boat.

BACON PIE

1 lb (450 grams) cooked bacon pieces
1 apple (peeled and cored)
1 onion
Salt and pepper
4 tablespoons medium dry cider
8 oz (225 grams) shortcrust pastry

Mince bacon, onion and apple, using a coarse cutter. Add cider and season to taste, if necessary. Roll out the pastry to fit a flan tin, spread bacon mixture over the top and cover with remaining pastry, decorating the top with pastry leaves. Brush with milk and bake in moderate oven approximately 30 minutes or until cooked.

BREAST OF LAMB
(Stuffed)

1 breast of lamb
4 oz (113 grams) sage and onion stuffing
1 oz (28 grams) flour
½ a stock cube
¼ pint (0.14 litre) medium dry cider
Salt and pepper
Sprig of Rosemary (optional)

Bone the lamb and remove the outer skin and some of the fat. Make the stuffing, spread it over the lamb and roll it up, using a tape or skewer to make it secure. Rub a little salt on the outside and place in a baking tin containing a knob of dripping previously made hot. Pour cider over the lamb and bake in moderate oven for about an hour and a quarter. If rosemary is used place it on the lamb before baking. Baste once or twice during cooking. When cooked remove to a hot dish and pour off any surplus fat. Crumble the stock cube into the gravy, thicken with the flour, adding a little more cider if necessary.

BAKED SAUSAGE MEAT

1 lb (454 grams) pork sausage meat
1 onion
1 cooking apple
1 oz (28 grams) flour
Salt and pepper
½ teaspoon mixed herbs
¼ pint (0.14 litre) dry cider
¼ teaspoon made mustard
Bay leaf (optional)

Shape sausage meat into flat cakes, toss in flour, place in greased casserole. Sprinkle with mixed herbs and smear mustard over each piece of sausage and cover with a layer of sliced onions and apple. Season with salt and pepper and pour cider over all. Cover with a lid and bake in moderate oven for approximately an hour and a quarter. When cooked thicken the gravy with a little flour, if necessary. If the bay leaf is used, place on top of sausage before baking.

CHICKEN RISOTTO

½ lb (225 grams) cooked chicken
4 oz (113 grams) Patna rice
½ pint (0.28 litre) white stock (chicken stock cube)
¼ pint (0.14 litre) medium dry cider
Clove of garlic
1 oz (28 grams) butter
1 tablespoon corn oil
Salt and pepper
1 small onion (chopped small)
Sliced tomatoes and green pepper for decoration

Wash and drain the rice. Heat butter and oil in frying pan, add onion and crushed garlic, fry lightly for a minute or two, do not brown. Add rice and stir until it is well coated with butter. Pour in the stock and cider, simmer 15 minutes. Season to taste. Cut the chicken into small pieces, add to the rice and heat through thoroughly. Turn into a serving dish and decorate with tomato and peppers.

This is a good basic risotto. Peas, beans, scraps of fish or meat can be added to make an economical lunch or supper dish.

COURGETTES

6 courgettes (cut in slices)
1 oz (28 grams) butter
1 tablespoon cooking oil
Salt and pepper
Wine glass of dry cider
Pinch of basil
Clove of garlic (crushed)

Heat butter and oil in frying pan, add crushed garlic and unpeeled, sliced courgettes. Cook for 5 minutes stirring a little, do not brown them. Add cider, basil, salt and pepper, cover with a lid and cook very gently until tender. Time taken depends on size of courgettes, 15 minutes is a good average time. Turn them into a serving dish and serve piping hot.

COD RAREBIT

¼ lb (113 grams) cooked cod
1 oz (28 grams) butter
2 tablespoons grated cheese
2 tablespoons dry cider

Melt butter in small saucepan, add cider and cheese, stir till the cheese melts. Flake the fish and mix with cheese mixture, seasoning to taste with freshly ground pepper and a little salt if necessary. Serve hot on toast.

CASSEROLED CHICKEN (WITH RICE)

2 legs of chicken
2 oz (57 grams) Patna rice
¼ pint (0.14 litre) dry cider
¼ pint (0.14 litre) white stock
Salt and pepper
2 sliced tomatoes
½ green pepper
1 onion
1 tablespoon cooking oil
1 oz (28 grams) butter

Heat oil and butter in pan, fry chicken both sides for a few minutes, place in a casserole. Sauté the onion, add rice and cook two minutes, add tomatoes, green pepper, cider, stock and seasoning. Transfer mixture to the casserole, stir it around a little, putting the chicken on top. Cover with a lid and cook in moderate oven for a little over an hour.

COURGETTES-au-GRATIN

6 courgettes (sliced lengthwise)
2 oz (56 grams) butter
Salt and pepper
Breadcrumbs
1 tablespoon of cooking oil
3 oz (84 grams) grated cheese
Clove of garlic (crushed)
1 oz (28 grams) flour
Wineglass of dry cider
¼ pint (0.14 litre) milk
Chopped parsley

Heat 1 oz (28 grams) butter and oil, add crushed garlic and courgettes. Cook 5 minutes, turning them over once; do not brown them. Add cider, salt and pepper and continue to cook for about 15 minutes until tender. Melt remaining butter in small saucepan, add flour and cook for 2 minutes. Gradually pour in the milk, beating well till smooth. Remove the courgettes to a serving dish, add remaining liquor to the sauce, blend altogether. Stir in 1 oz (28 grams) of cheese and when it has melted pour sauce over courgettes. Sprinkle top with remaining cheese and a tablespoon of bread-crumbs. Brown under a grill for a few minutes. Garnish with chopped parsley.

CIDER STUFFING

4 oz (113 grams) stale bread
Wineglass dry cider
1 tablespoonful melted butter
Small minced onion
Teaspoon minced onion
Teaspoon mixed herbs (level)
Salt and pepper
Egg yolk

Remove crusts from bread and soak it in cider for 10 minutes. Squeeze the bread if necessary and place in a basin. Add remaining ingredients and use as required. This is a basic recipe, sage can be used for pork, parsley and thyme for fish or chicken. If the stuffing is served separately place it in a small greased dish and cook in moderate oven 15 minutes.

CIDER SAUCE (SAVOURY)

1 oz (28 grams) butter
1 oz (28 grams) flour
Garlic powder
1 teaspoon lemon juice
½ pint (0.14 litre) dry cider
Salt and pepper
Level teaspoon sugar
1 dessertspoon chopped capers

Melt butter in saucepan, add flour and cook a minute or two. Pour in the cider and lemon juice, add a liberal shake of garlic and the sugar. Beat well and cook for a further four minutes or until smooth. Season with salt and pepper and stir in the capers. Particularly good with fish.

CREAMED HAM (WITH CIDER)

¾ lb (340 grams) cooked minced ham
1 tablespoon plain flour
1 oz (28 grams) margarine
Small packet frozen vegetables
½ a tumblerful dry cider
¼ pint (0.14 litre) milk

Mince the ham and cook the vegetables. Melt margarine in saucepan, add flour to form a roux. Gradually add milk and cook for a few minutes till thick and smooth, remove from heat. Stir in the cider, using sufficient to make it creamy but not too thin. Add ham and cooked vegetables, season to taste. Reheat but do not boil.

FISH FINGERS

1 lb (454 grams) filleted coley
½ lb (227 grams) mashed potatoes
1 oz (28 grams) margarine
1 pint (0.14 litre) dry cider
1 egg (small size)
Salt and pepper
Teaspoon finely chopped parsley
Golden crumbs (packet)

Poach fish in cider until it flakes, approximately 15 minutes. Drain off the liquid and place fish in a basin with remaining ingredients, seasoning it fairly well. Mix well and place it in a shallow baking tin. Sprinkle with golden crumbs and cut into fingers. Bake in moderate oven for 20 minutes until brown. The liquid can be thickened with a level teaspoon of cornflour to make a pleasing sauce.

PIQUANT HERRINGS

2 fresh herrings
¼ pint (0.14 litre) dry cider
Pinch of fennel
1 tablespoon vegetable oil
3 peppercorns

72

1 shallot
Salt and pepper
2 gherkins (chopped small)

Wash and fillet the herrings. Place in a frying pan with other ingredients and poach uncovered for 15 minutes, turning them over once. These herrings can be left in the liquor until cold and served with salad.

STUFFED HERRINGS

2 large herrings
¼ pint (0.14 litre) dry cider
Cider stuffing (as recipe)
1 oz (28 grams) butter
Salt and pepper

Prepare and fillet herrings. Place a spoonful of stuffing on each fillet and fold it over, put into a buttered ovenproof dish. Pour over the cider, season to taste and dot the butter over all. Cover with a lid and bake in moderate oven for 20 minutes, or until cooked.

TASTY LIVER BAKE

½ lb (227 grams) pigs liver
4 rashers of streaky bacon
1 onion
Dessertspoonful flour
2 tablespoons corn oil or dripping
¼ pint (0.14 litre) medium dry cider
2 tomatoes
Salt, pepper and oregano
Parsley for garnish

Soak liver in cider for 1 hour. Drain well and toss in flour to which a little salt and pepper has been added. Heat oil in pan and lightly fry the liver, one minute each side. Place on a layer of sliced onions in a casserole, season with salt, pepper and a pinch of oregano. Cover with derinded rashers of bacon. To the remaining oil in pan, mix in the flour and gradually add cider. Bring to the boil and pour over the liver. Cover with a lid and cook in slow oven for 1½ hours. When cooked arrange liver and bacon on a serving dish and strain the gravy over the top. Decorate with tomatoes, return it to the oven for a minute or two and serve garnished with parsley.

This dish can be cooked on top of the stove if preferred. Toss liver in seasoned flour, fry with bacon and onions till tender and brown, arrange on serving dish. To the oil in pan, mix in flour and cider, cook three minutes, and strain over liver. Decorate with tomatoes and parsley.

GAMMON AND CIDER

2 gammon steaks
1 onion
1 tablespoon cooking oil
Bouquet garni
¼ pint (0.14 litre) dry cider
Shake of garlic granules
1 tablespoon sugar (level spoon)
Salt and pepper

Bring to the boil the cider, oil, sugar and sliced onion, simmer for a few minutes without a lid to reduce it a little. Snip round the outside of the gammon steaks and put them into an ovenproof dish. Sprinkle with pepper, garlic and a very little salt. Place the bouquet garni on top, add cider, cover with a lid and cook in a moderate oven for ¾ hour.

LAMB CRUMBLE

1 lb (454 grams) boneless lamb
1 large onion
Small tin of tomatoes
4 oz (113 grams) breadcrumbs
Salt and pepper
2 oz (57 grams) mushrooms
¼ pint (0.14 litre) dry cider
¼ pint (0.14 litre) stock cube

74

Cut lamb into small pieces and toss in flour, place in greased casserole. Cover with a layer of onions, mushrooms and the tomatoes, including the juice. Season to taste. Bring to the boil the cider and stock and reduce it a little, pour over all. Cover with breadcrumbs and bake in moderate oven approximately one and a quarter hours or until the lamb is tender and the crumbs brown and crisp.

PORK HOT POT

4 slices belly of pork
¼ pint (0.14 litre) medium dry cider
2 onions
1 lb (454 grams) sliced potatoes
1 apple
1 oz (28 grams) melted butter
Pinch of sage
Salt and pepper

Place two slices of pork in a casserole, cover with a layer of sliced onion and apple. Sprinkle with a little sage, salt and pepper. Add remaining slices of pork, onion and apple. Pour in the cider and cover with sliced potatoes. Sprinkle with a little more salt and pepper and brush with melted butter. Cover with a lid and cook in moderate oven for ¾ hour. Remove the lid and continue to cook until the potatoes are crisp and brown.

The pork can be cut into small pieces if preferred.

PORC A L'ORANGE

1½ lb (680 grams) lean pork
1 onion and a clove or garlic
2 tablespoons cooking oil
1 pint (0.56 litre) stock cube
1 large onion
1 tablespoon cornflour
¼ pint (0.14 litre) dry cider
Salt and pepper

Cut pork into small pieces and toss in cornflour. Heat oil in pan, fry onion and crushed garlic for a minute or two then add the meat and brown a little. Transfer to casserole with stock, cider, juice of the orange plus a little grated rind. Add seasoning and remaining cornflour. Cover with a lid and cook in moderate oven approximately 2 hours. Whilst this is cooking, remove pith from remaining peel, cut it into very fine strips, cover with water and bring to the boil. Use to garnish the pork before serving.

SWEET APPLE COOKIES

4 oz (113 grams) margarine
4 oz (113 grams) caster sugar
6 oz (170 grams) self raising flour
2 eggs
2 tablespoons grated apple
Level teaspoon mixed spice
1 tablespoon chopped walnuts
Sweet cider to mix

Mix together flour, sugar and spice, rub in the margarine, add apple and walnuts. Add well beaten eggs and sufficient cider to give a dropping consistency, and put into paper case. Bake in moderately hot oven for 15 minutes. When cold these cookies can be iced with glacé icing and topped with half a walnut.

APPLE CRUMBLE

1 lb (454 grams) cooking apples
Sugar to taste
Wineglass of cider
Pinch of ginger
1 oz (28 grams) sugar
2 oz (57 grams) margarine
4 oz (113 grams) flour

Prepare apples and cut into thick slices, place in greased pie dish, sprinkle with sugar and ginger and pour in the cider. Rub together the sugar, margarine and flour until it resembles breadcrumbs, and scatter over the apples. Sprinkle a little sugar over the top and bake in moderate oven about 35 minutes or until the apples are cooked and the top crisp and brown.

APPLE FRITTERS

1 or 2 cooking apples
Caster sugar
Hot oil for frying
4 oz (113 grams) flour
1 egg
1 teaspoon olive oil
Sweet cider

Peel and core the apples, cut into rings. Mix the flour with egg, oil and sufficient cider to make a thick smooth batter. Dip apple rings in sugar then batter. Fry in hot oil until crisp and brown. Drain on a wire tray and sprinkle with caster sugar.

APPLE CAKE

½ lb (227 grams) S.R. flour
¼ lb (113 grams) margarine
¼ lb (113 grams) caster sugar
2 eggs
Small pinch of salt
A little milk to mix
2 medium size cooking apples (grated)
2 oz (58 grams) sultanas
2 tablespoons mixed peel
1 heaped tablespoon chopped walnut
1 level teaspoon mixed spice

Combine all dry ingredients in bowl, rub in margarine until it resembles breadcrumbs. Add grated apple, beaten eggs and sufficient milk to make a dropping consistency. Turn into a well greased tin, sprinkle liberally with granulated sugar and bake in moderate oven for approximately an hour.

APPLE SPONGE

½ lb (227 grams) Bramley cooking apples
2 tablespoons granulated sugar
Level teaspoon mixed spice
¼ lb (113 grams) margarine
¼ lb (113 grams) caster sugar
6 oz (170 grams) S.R. flour
2 eggs
Milk to mix

Rub fat into flour and sugar. Mix with well beaten eggs and sufficient milk to make a dropping consistency. Peel apples and cut into thin slices. Place sponge mixture in a greased tin or dish, put apple slices on top, slightly overlapping each other. Sprinkle with sugar and spice. Bake in moderate oven for approximately 35-40 minutes.

BUN LOAF

8 oz (227 grams) plain flour
1 oz (28 grams) lard
Pinch of salt
1 egg
½ oz (14 grams) fresh yeast
1 oz (28 grams) mixed peel
1 oz (28 grams) sugar
3 oz (84 grams) sultanas
Tablespoon marmalade
½ teaspoon cinnamon
Pinch of nutmeg
4 tablespoons warm water
Sweet cider to mix

Mix yeast with warm water. Leave 10 minutes until it begins to bubble. Sieve flour and salt, rub in the lard, add fruit, sugar and spices. Add yeast, beaten egg and marmalade and mix with sufficient cider to make a fairly soft dough. Transfer to a floured board and knead for a minute or two. Put into a warm greased loaf tin and keep in a warm place until the dough doubles its bulk and reaches the top of the tin. Bake in a moderate oven approximately 35 minutes. If a glazed top is preferred, brush the top with a little sugar syrup when taken from the oven. To make this boil 2 tablespoons of sugar with a tablespoon of water till sugar is dissolved, (about a minute). Cool on a wire tray and when cold, slice and spread generously with butter.

BANANA DESSERT

3 bananas
1 oz (28 grams) butter
1 oz (28 grams) Demerara sugar
Wineglass medium dry cider

Melt butter in pan, add sugar and cider, stirring continuously until the sugar has dissolved. Add sliced bananas and cook over very low heat for 3 or 4 minutes.

CIDER SAUCE (SWEET)

1 oz (28 grams) butter
1 oz (28 grams) flour
½ pint (0.28 litre) sweet cider
1 heaped tablespoon sugar
½ teaspoon mixed cinnamon and nutmeg
2 tablespoons thin cream

Melt butter in small saucepan, add flour and cook 2 minutes. Gradually pour in the cider and mix well. Add sugar and spices and whip vigorously. Remove from heat and add cream. This sauce is suitable for steamed fruit puddings.

CIDER AND ORANGE SAUCE

2 oz (57 grams) butter
2 heaped tablespoons sugar
¼ pint (0.14 litre) cider
Juice and grated rind of orange

Melt butter in small saucepan, add sugar, juice and rind. When sugar has dissolved gradually add cider. Simmer over very low heat for a minute or two. This is particularly good for reheating slices of Christmas pudding, or poured over pancakes.

FRANGIPANI TART

6 oz (170 grams) shortcrust pastry
¼ pint (0.14 litre) medium sweet cider
6 oz (170 grams) mixed fruit
1 oz (28 grams) brown sugar
2 teaspoons cornflour
Glacé icing

Make pastry, line a flan tin and bake blind. Place washed fruit in a saucepan with sugar, cider and butter, boil 5 minutes. Mix cornflour with a tablespoon of cider to a smooth cream. Add to boiling fruit and cook for a minute until it thickens. Pour fruit into the pastry case and when cold run a thin layer of icing sugar over the top.

PRUNES AND CIDER

½ lb (227 grams) prunes
½ pint (0.28 litre) sweet cider
2 level tablespoons sugar
1 teaspoon lemon juice (optional)

Wash prunes and soak overnight in cider and lemon juice. Simmer gently till tender. Add sugar and leave covered till cold. Adding sugar at the last moment ensures that the skins remain soft.

PRUNE FOOL

½ lb (227 grams) prunes
½ pint (0.28 litre) sweet cider
½ pint (0.28 litre) fairly thick custard
2 level tablespoons sugar

Cook prunes as previous recipe, leave to get cold then remove the stones. Liquidise until pureed, add warm custard and whip well. Serve cold with cream.

FARMHOUSE BREAD PUDDING

¾ lb (340 grams) stale bread
2 oz (57 grams) melted lard
2 oz (57 grams) brown sugar
4 oz (113 grams) mixed dried fruit
¼ pint (0.14 litre) sweet cider
2 oz (57 grams) mixed peel
2 teaspoons mixed spice
1 large egg

Remove crust from bread, break into pieces and soak in cider for 15 minutes. Strain off any surplus cider and break the bread with a fork. Add fruit, sugar peel and spice. Mix with beaten egg and melted lard. Place in a greased pie dish and bake in moderate oven for approximately 1 hour or until brown and set. Turn it out and sprinkle thickly with sugar.

". . . 'fraid I overdid the cider in the pudding, dear . . ."

FRUIT AND RICE PUDDING

6 oz (170 grams) cold cooked rice
2 oz (57 grams) sugar
1 oz (28 grams) sultanas
¾ lb (340 grams) Bramley apples
1 teaspoon cinnamon
Knob of butter
Wineglass sweet cider
1 teaspoon brown sugar

Butter a pie dish, place a layer of rice covered by a layer of apples and sugar, sprinkle with a little cinnamon and some of the sultanas. Continue in this fashion until all the ingredients are used. Pour over the cider, sprinkle with brown sugar and dot with the butter. Cook in moderate oven 40 minutes.

PEARS AND RICE

1 lb (454 grams) dessert pears
2 oz (57 grams) sugar
¼ pint (0.14 litre) medium dry cider
4 oz (113 grams) rice
1 pint (0.56 litre) milk
2 tablespoons apricot jam
Glacé cherries

Peel and core pears, cut in halves. Poach gently in the cider with 1 oz of sugar for a few minutes until soft but not mushy, time taken depends on the type of pears used. Cook rice in milk with remaining 1 oz of sugar approximately 15 minutes until soft and the milk absorbed. Transfer rice to a serving dish, strain the pears and place on top of rice. Mix apricot jam with juice from pears and bring to the boil. Boil hard for 1 or 2 minutes without a lid to reduce and pour it over the pears. Decorate with cherries.

CHAPTER 10

My Favourite Apple Recipes

APPLE CHUTNEY

3 lb (1½ kilos) cooking apples
1 lb (454 grams) onions
¾ lb (340 grams) brown sugar
4 oz (113 grams) dates
Clove of garlic (optional)
1 pint (0.56 litre) vinegar
Level teaspoon mixed spice
½ teaspoon curry powder
Pinch of ground ginger
Salt and pepper

Mince apples, onions and dates. Place in pan with vinegar, sugar, garlic and spices. Season with salt and pepper and simmer for approximately 25 minutes or until the required consistency is obtained.

APPLE CHEESE

3 lb (1½ kilos) cooking apples
¼ teaspoon ground cloves
1 lb (454 grams) sugar to each lb apple pulp
¼ teaspoon mixed spice
1½ pints (0.84 litres) water

Wash the apples and cut roughly. Place in pan with water and spices, simmer till soft, rub through a nylon sieve. Weigh the pulp and put it into a saucepan with the sugar. Bring slowly to the boil, stirring to allow the sugar to melt. Continue to cook until thick, approximately 35 minutes.

APPLE BATTER

2 large cooking apples
2 level tablespoons brown sugar
1 tablespoon sultanas
1 oz (28 grams) lard
4 oz (113 grams) plain flour
1 egg
½ pint (0.28 litre) milk
½ teaspoon mixed spice (optional)

Make batter by mixing flour, egg and milk. Beat well and allow to stand 1 hour. Peel and core apples and cut into thick slices. Heat fat in a baking tin, pour in the batter mixture and quickly place apple slices on top. Scatter the sultanas and sugar overall and bake in quick oven for 15 minutes, reducing the heat to moderate for a further 25 minutes, or until brown and well risen. If the mixed spice is used sprinkle over sultanas and sugar. This is very good served with syrup sauce, made as follows.

Syrup Sauce
½ pint (0.28 litre) water
3 oz (84 grams) golden syrup
Teaspoon lemon juice
Level dessertspoon cornflour

Mix cornflour with a tablespoon of water, put the remainder in a small saucepan with the syrup and lemon juice. Bring to the boil and stir in the blended cornflour. Cook for a minute or two till the sauce is smooth and fairly clear.

APPLE AND DATE TART

8oz (227 grams) shortcrust pastry
2 large cooking apples (Bramleys if possible)

4 oz (113 grams) chopped dates
3 oz (84 grams) icing sugar
1 tablespoon Demerara sugar
½ teaspoon mixed spice

Make pastry, roll out half to fit a flan tin. Cover with sliced apples, dates, sugar and spice. Cover with remaining pastry and bake in moderate oven for 40 minutes or until cooked. When nearly cold, coat the top with glacé icing made with the icing sugar and a little water.

CRAB APPLE JELLY

4 lb (2 kilos) John Downie crab apples
2 pints (1.12 litres) water
1 lb (454 grams) sugar to each pint of juice
A few strips of lemon peel; do not use any pith

Wash and cut up the fruit (without peeling) place in saucepan with water and lemon peel. Simmer for about ¾ hour, keeping a lid on the pan. Strain through a jelly bag until all liquid is extracted. Return juice to a saucepan, bring it to the boil and add 1 pound of sugar to each pint of juice. Boil rapidly until the setting point is reached. Test after 10 minutes by placing a little on a saucer, if it wrinkles when cold it is boiled sufficiently.

APPLE AND BLACKBERRY JELLY

3 lb (1½ kilos) apples
3 lb (1½ kilos) blackberries
1 lb (454 grams) sugar to each pint of juice
6 cloves
2 pints (1.12 litres) water

Wash and cut up the apples (without peeling) and place in pan with other ingredients except sugar. Bring to the boil and simmer approximately ¾ hour or until the fruit is well broken down and quite soft. Strain through a jelly bag and measure the juice. Return it to a saucepan and bring it to the boil. Add a pound of sugar to each pint of juice, stir till dissolved and boil rapidly for 10 minutes until the setting point is reached. Any scum rising to the surface should be removed when setting point is reached. The jelly should be placed in warm jars as soon as possible and whilst still hot, covered with circles of waxed paper. Tie down when completely cold.

FARMHOUSE TART

1 lb (454 grams) cooking apples
2 oz (57 grams) sugar
8 oz (227 grams) shortcrust pastry
½ pint (0.28 litre) custard
2 tablespoons red jam
1 tablespoon of dessicated coconut

Roll out the pastry to fit a flan case and bake blind. Prepare apples and cook with sugar and just enough water to prevent burning. Remove from heat and leave to get cold. Spread jam over the cold pastry case and cover with apple. Make custard and pour over the top, making sure it reaches the edges of the pastry as it shrinks a little when cold. Decorate with coconut or as desired.

PORK CHOPS

2 pork chops
2 tomatoes (skinned)
¼ lb (113 grams) onions (sliced)
1 tablespoon cooking oil
¼ pint (0.14 litre) stock
¼ lb (113 grams) sharp cooking apples
¼ lb (113 grams) button mushrooms
Teaspoon flour
Salt, pepper and bayleaf

Heat oil in frying pan, sauté onion and chops for a few minutes. Place a layer of apples, mushroom and tomatoes in bottom of casserole. Remove chops and onion from pan and put on top of vegetables. Season to taste. Mix the flour in remaining fat, stir a little, add the stock. When blended pour over the chops and place the bayleaf on top. Cover with a lid and cook in moderate oven for about an hour. Gammon steaks can be used instead of pork chops, remove the rind before cooking or snip it in several places to prevent it curling as it cooks.

MY WAY OF PREPARING BRIDGE ROLLS

Bridge rolls, Ham, Watercress, Lettuce, Salt, Butter.

With a sharp knife cut a slit down the middle of each roll, making sure you do not cut right through. Open it slightly, spread with butter. Place a piece of lettuce in each, sprinkle with salt. Add a small roll of ham and place a sprig of watercress at each end. Placed on a large dish and garnished with salading these look most attractive.

WELSH RAREBIT FINGERS

8 oz (227 grams) Cheddar cheese
1 wineglass cider
Slices of toast (crusts removed)
½ teaspoon made mustard
Pepper
Worcestershire sauce

Grate cheese, put into a small saucepan with mustard, pepper, cider and sauce. Cook till smooth, stirring continually. Spread on toast, place under a grill for a few minutes, then cut into fingers. A dish of these can be covered in foil and kept warm in an oven until required.

MEAT LOAF

1 lb (454 grams) minced beef
1 lb (454 grams) sausage-meat
1 grated onion
Worcestershire sauce
½ teaspoon mixed herbs
Salt & pepper

2 oz (57 grams) fine breadcrumbs
1 egg
1 dessertspoon tomato puree
4 tablespoons cider or stock

Combine all ingredients, season fairly well. Pack into a lightly greased loaf tin and place in baking tin containing about an inch of water. Bake in moderate oven, about 1½ hours, middle shelf. When cooked, pour off surplus fat, leave five minutes then turn it out onto a serving dish. Slice and serve hot on bread toasted on one side only. Can also be served cold with salad.

QUICK SAUSAGE-MEAT DUNKS

1 lb (454 grams) pork sausage-meat
Packet Golden Crumbs
Pinch of sage
Hot tomato sauce for dunking
Salt & pepper
1 Small beaten egg
Finely chopped onion
Hot oil for frying

Mix sausage-meat with sage, onion, salt and pepper. Form into very small balls. Dip in beaten egg and golden crumbs. Fry gently in hot oil until brown. Insert a cocktail stick and serve with a bowl of hot tomato sauce.

A tin of Campbells Condensed tomato soup, heated with two tablespoons dry cider, makes a quick and easy sauce.

SNACKS FOR CIDER PARTIES

I consider snacks for cider parties, which are popular in the West Country, should be more substantial than those prepared for wine and cheese parties. Ploughman's suppers are great favourites and usually consist of home-made rolls, cheese, lettuce, tomatoes, chutney or pickled onions plus butter. I have included in this chapter recipes for snacks I enjoy with cider. The method I use for making rolls is quite simple, the quantity I use makes about 14 rolls.

EASY RECIPE FOR ROLLS

1 lb (454 grams) wholemeal flour
½ lb (227 grams) strong white bread flour
1 sachet Homepride Harvest Gold yeast
¾ pint (427ml) warm water
1½ teaspoons salt
⅛ teaspoon sugar
1 oz (28 grams) lard

Sieve flour into a large basin, add salt and sugar then rub in the lard. Shake in the yeast (dry), mix a little. Add the warm water all at once, mix until it forms a dough, transfer to floured board and knead thoroughly. Shape into rolls and place them on greased baking tin. Allow to rise until they have doubled in size. Bake in hot oven 20 minutes. If shiny rolls are required, brush with milk or white of egg before baking. I prefer not to have them glazed.

CIDER BATTER SAVOURIES

Batter Mix
4 oz (113 grams) plain flour
Pinch of salt
¼ pint (0.14 litre) dry cider
1 egg
1 dessertspoon olive oil

Sieve flour and salt, add egg and oil. Beat well then gradually add the cider to make a smooth thick batter. Dip any of the following in batter and fry in hot deep fat or oil until brown: Cocktail sausages, Frankfurters, tinned meat squares, small cheese sandwiches, ham sandwiches (cut into fingers), pieces of left over chicken.

SAVOURY MEAT BALLS

1 lb (454 grams) minced beef
Salt & pepper
1 teaspoon mixed herbs
1 small egg

¼ pint (142 ml) brown stock (cube)
1 tablespoon flour
1 tablespoon cooking oil
1 heaped tablespoon breadcrumbs
1 small onion
1 dessertspoon condensed tomato puree
¼ pint (142 ml) dry cider

Grate onion, put into a basin with meat, puree, herbs, bread-crumbs, salt and pepper. Mix with sufficient egg to bind and using wet hands make into small balls (bite size). Place in fridge for an hour. Heat oil in large shallow pan, fry a little more onion until soft. Mix in the flour, then gradually add the stock and cider. Cook for a few minutes, add the meat balls and cook slowly approximately 20 minutes. Remove meat balls from pan using a slotted spoon, place on large tray, put a cocktail stick in each and serve hot.

POTATO PORKERS

1 lb (454 grams) pork chipolata sausages
½ lb (227 grams) fried onions
8 medium size potatoes baked in their jackets
1 small Bramley cooking apple
1 level tablespoon plain flour
Salt & pepper
1 teaspoon tomato puree
1 small chopped onion
¼ pint (142 ml) dry cider

Cook sausages in a little fat or oil until brown, remove from pan. Cook the small onion and apple in remaining fat until soft, add flour and tomato puree, mix well then gradually pour in the cider. Cook for a few minutes until smooth, add sausages and simmer 10 minutes. Cut the baked potatoes in halves, make a slight groove on the top and put in a few fried onions. Top with a sausage and pour a little sauce over each. Serve hot.

APPLES FOR THE FREEZER

Apples freeze very well, windfalls especially being suitable for this purpose. Peel apples, cut in slices and place immediately in salted water. When a sufficient quantity of apples are prepared, rinse in cold water, drain well and pack in freezer bags. Place in freezer as soon as possible. I have stored apples in this way for eight months and when removed from freezer they are as white as fresh apples. The amount of salt I use for the brine is 1 tablespoon to 1¼ pints of water.

Apple puree is also useful. Prepare apples, cut in quarters and stew with a very little water and sugar to taste. Pour into containers, allowing half an inch headroom. Allow to get completely cold before placing in the freezer.

Apples improve many savoury dishes; try frying sliced apples with sausages.

Mix grated apple with sage and onion stuffing to serve with pork.

Use a little apple when preparing curries.

Apple sauce is well known, cooked with cider instead of water makes it even better.

Add a tablespoon of gelatine (previously soaked in a little cold water) to ½ pint of sweetened apple puree. Place in small containers and when cold serve with cold roast pork.

Sprinkle a dessertspoon of finely chopped mint to the above ingredients.

Acknowledgements

I wish to thank the Cider Museum, Hereford and Bulmers Ltd, Hereford for the information and photographs they kindly sent to me. Also Brewmaker of Southampton and Walker Desmond and Sons Ltd. of Stockport for their excellent photographs and Mr. D. Pearman (Loftus).

Appendix 1

Commercial cidermaking sources the author has either visited or had recommended to her by friends.

Ashill Cider:
Ashill Farm,
Nr. Ilminster,
Somerset.

Brympton D'Evercy Cider:
Brympton D'Evercy,
Yeovil,
Somerset.

Bulmers Cider:
H.P. Bulmer,
Plough Lane,
Hereford.

Burrow Mill Cider:
Pass Vale Farm,
Kingsbury Episcopi,
Martock,
Somerset.

Cider Makers:
High Farm,
Mudford,
Nr. Yeovil,
Somerset.

Coates Gaymers Cider:
Kilver Street,
Shepton Mallet,
Somerset.

Compton Manor Farm Cider:
Compton Manor Farm,
Over Compton,
Sherborne,
Dorset.

Country Fayre Cider:
West Stoughton,
Wedmore,
Somerset.

English Cider Centre:
Middle Farm,
Firle,
Lewes,
East Sussex.

Godshill Farm Cider:
The Cider Barn,
Godshill,
Isle of Wight.

Grays Farm Cider:
Halstow,
Tedbury St. Mary,
Exeter,
Devon.

Halls Cider:
Wistaria Farm,
Fordgate,
Bridgwater,
Somerset.

Hancocks Cider:
Clapworthy Mill,
Nr. South Moulton,
Devon.

Hecks Farmhouse Cider:
11 Middle Leigh,
Street,
Somerset.

Inch's Cider:
Hatherleigh Road,
Winkleigh,
Devon.

Long Ashton Cider:
Long Ashton Research Station,
Long Ashton,
Bristol,
Avon.

Luscombe Cider:
Luscombe Farm,
Buckfastleigh,
Devon.

Meadowsweet Cider:
Meadowsweet Farm,
Bicknoller,
Taunton,
Somerset.

Merrydown Strong Cider:
Horam Manor,
Horam,
Heathfield,
East Sussex.

Gillian Pearks:
Yearlstone Cider,
Yearlstone House,
Bickleigh,
Devon.

Pepe & Son:
Newton Road,
Scotts Bridge,
Torquay,
Devon.

Perry's Cider:
Cider Mill,
Orchardlands,
Dowlish Wake,
Devon.

Pippinfield Cider & Wines:
Harepath Hill,
Seaton,
Devon.

Raymond Cider:
Woodcote Farm,
Crewkerne Road,
Hawkchurch,
Devon.

Senlac Cider:
Carr Taylor Vineyards,
Westfield,
Hastings,
East Sussex.

Sheppy's Cider:
Three Bridges,
Bradford on Tone,
Taunton,
Somerset.

Taunton Cider:
Taunton Cider Company,
Norton Fitzwarren,
Taunton,
Somerset.

Whiteways Cider:
Whimple,
Devon.

Wolfeton Cider:
Wolfeton House,
Dorchester,
Dorset.

Wonnacots of Bude:
Cider Makers,
2, Lansdown Road,
Bude,
Cornwall.

Appendix 2

Apples the author has often used for cider making. A blend of cider and other apples will produce quite a good drinkable cider.

Breakwells Seedling	Mildy sharp, soft flesh, slightly astringent.
Brown Snout	Medium size fruit; bitter sweet – early November
Chisel Jersey	Hard, medium size fruit, bitter sweet, astringent.
Cox's Orange	Premier dessert apple. Orange colour, yellow flesh, sweet and juicy. Late season.
Crispins	Large yellowish green apple, juicy with good flavour. Late season.
Dabinette	Cider apple. Small to medium size fruit, bitter-sweet. Mid season.
Fillbarrel	High tannin, low acid, bitter sweet.
Golden Delicious	Fleshy apple, large and juicy. Two types, green and red. Useful for blending.
John Downie	Small crabapple. Scarlet and yellow colour. Acid. Good for blending.
Kingston Blacks	Excellent cider apple. Dark red colour. Old Somerset apple.
Morgans Sweet	Early variety, sweet, moderate tannin.
Newton Wonder	Medium round apple, brownish yellow skin, good flavour, sub acid.

Somerset Redstreak	Medium size fruit, bitter-sweet, mid-season.
Sweet Coppin	Sweet, low acid and tannin, medium size fruit.
Tom Putts	Declined over the past years. Good for cider although it is a culinary apple. Yellow streaked red, juicy, crisp and acid.
Tramletts Bitter	Good cider apple, medium size, high tannin, early season.
Rev. W. Wilks	Culinary, good flavour, large greenish yellow apple.
Yarlington Mill	Medium size apple, bitter sweet, high tannin, low acid. Good cider apple.

Some varieties of pears are excellent for blending with apples with a high acid content.

Beurre Hardy	October variety. Large fruit, good flavour. Skins contain tannin.
Comice	Sweet, good flavour, juicy, skins contain tannin. November-December.
Conference	Medium size, sweet and juicy, skins contain a certain amount of tannin. October-February.
Perry Pears (if available)	Very astringent and hard.

94

INDEX